COLOR YOUR
CIVIL WAR

FEATURING ART BY
STEVE MCNIVEN & DEXTER VINES,
RON GARNEY & BILL REINHOLD,
ALEX MALEEV, LEINIL YU,
JIM CHEUNG & LIVESAY, MICHAEL TURNER,
ROBERTO DE LA TORRE & JON SIBAL,
JEREMY HAUN & MARK MORALES AND
PATRICK ZIRCHER & SCOTT HANNA

COLLECTION EDITOR: JENNIFER GRÜNWALD
ASSOCIATE EDITOR: SARAH BRUNSTAD
ASSOCIATE MANAGING EDITOR: ALEX STARBUCK
EDITOR, SPECIAL PROJECTS: MARK D. BEAZLEY
VP, PRODUCTION & SPECIAL PROJECTS: JEFF YOUNGQUIST
SVP PRINT, SALES & MARKETING: DAVID GABRIEL
BOOK DESIGNER: JAY BOWEN

EDITOR IN CHIEF: AXEL ALONSO
CHIEF CREATIVE OFFICER: JOE QUESADA
PUBLISHER: DAN BUCKLEY
EXECUTIVE PRODUCER: ALAN FINE

COLOR YOUR OWN CIVIL WAR. First printing 2016. ISBN# 978-0-7851-9559-7. Published by MARVEL WORLDWIDE, INC., a subsidiary of MARVEL ENTERTAINMENT, LLC. OFFICE OF PUBLICATION: 135 West 50th Street, New York, NY 10020. Copyright © 2016 MARVEL No similarity between any of the names, characters, persons, and/or institutions in this magazine with those of any living or dead person or institution is intended, and any such similarity which may exist is purely coincidental. **Printed in the U.S.A.** ALAN FINE, President, Marvel Entertainment; DAN BUCKLEY, President, TV, Publishing & Brand Management; JOE QUESADA, Chief Creative Officer; TOM BREVOORT, SVP of Publishing; DAVID BOGART, SVP of Business Affairs & Operations, Publishing & Partnership; C.B. CEBULSKI, VP of Brand Management & Development, Asia; DAVID GABRIEL, SVP of Sales & Marketing, Publishing; JEFF YOUNGQUIST, VP of Production & Special Projects; DAN CARR, Executive Director of Publishing Technology; ALEX MORALES, Director of Publishing Operations; SUSAN CRESPI, Production Manager; STAN LEE, Chairman Emeritus. For information regarding advertising in Marvel Comics or on Marvel.com, please contact Vit DeBellis, Integrated Sales Manager, at vdebellis@marvel.com. For Marvel subscription inquiries, please call 888-511-5480. **Manufactured between 2/5/2016 and 3/14/2016 by SHERIDAN, CHELSEA, MI, USA.**

10 9 8 7 6 5 4 3 2 1

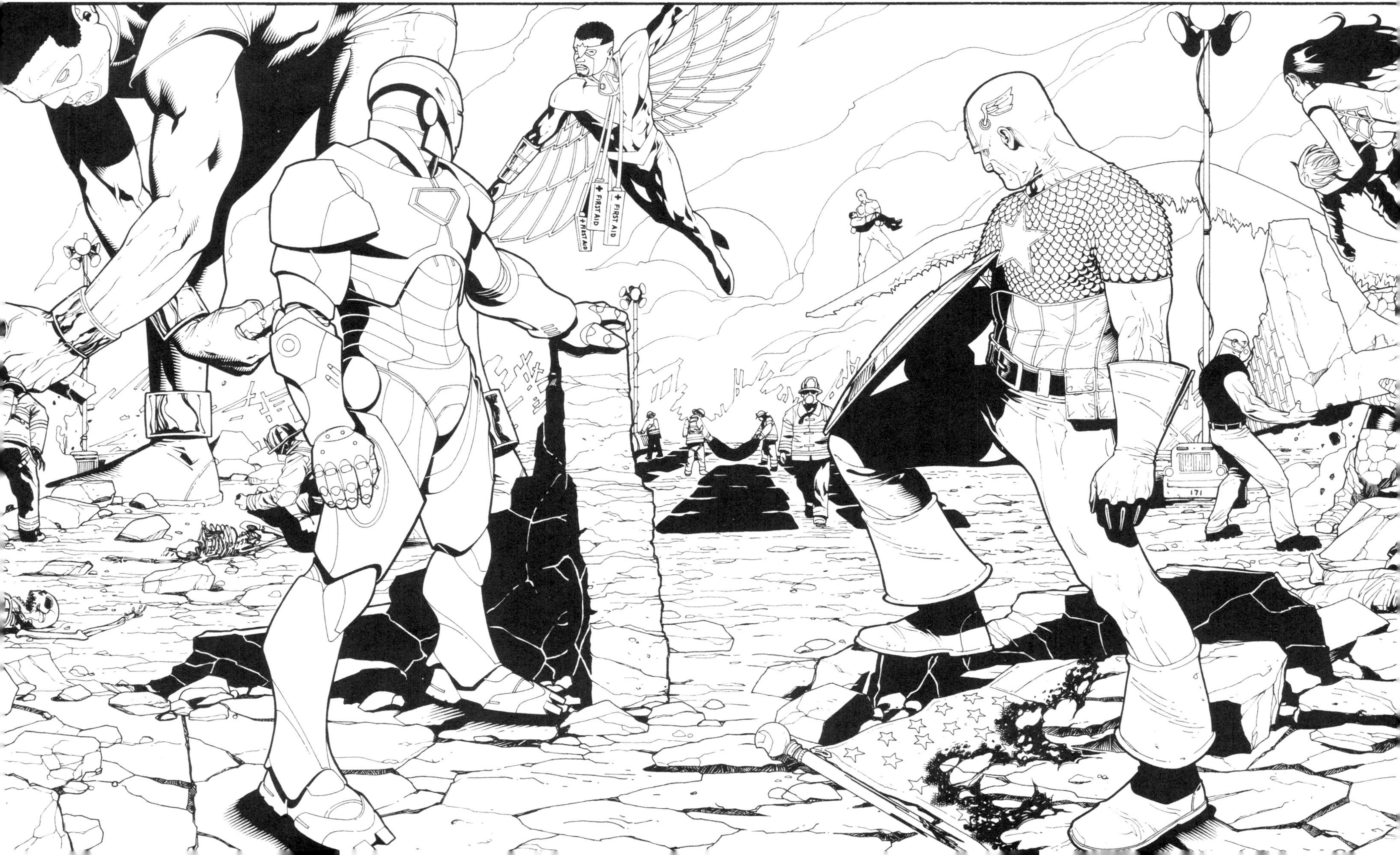
FIRST AID
FIRST AID
FIRST AID
171

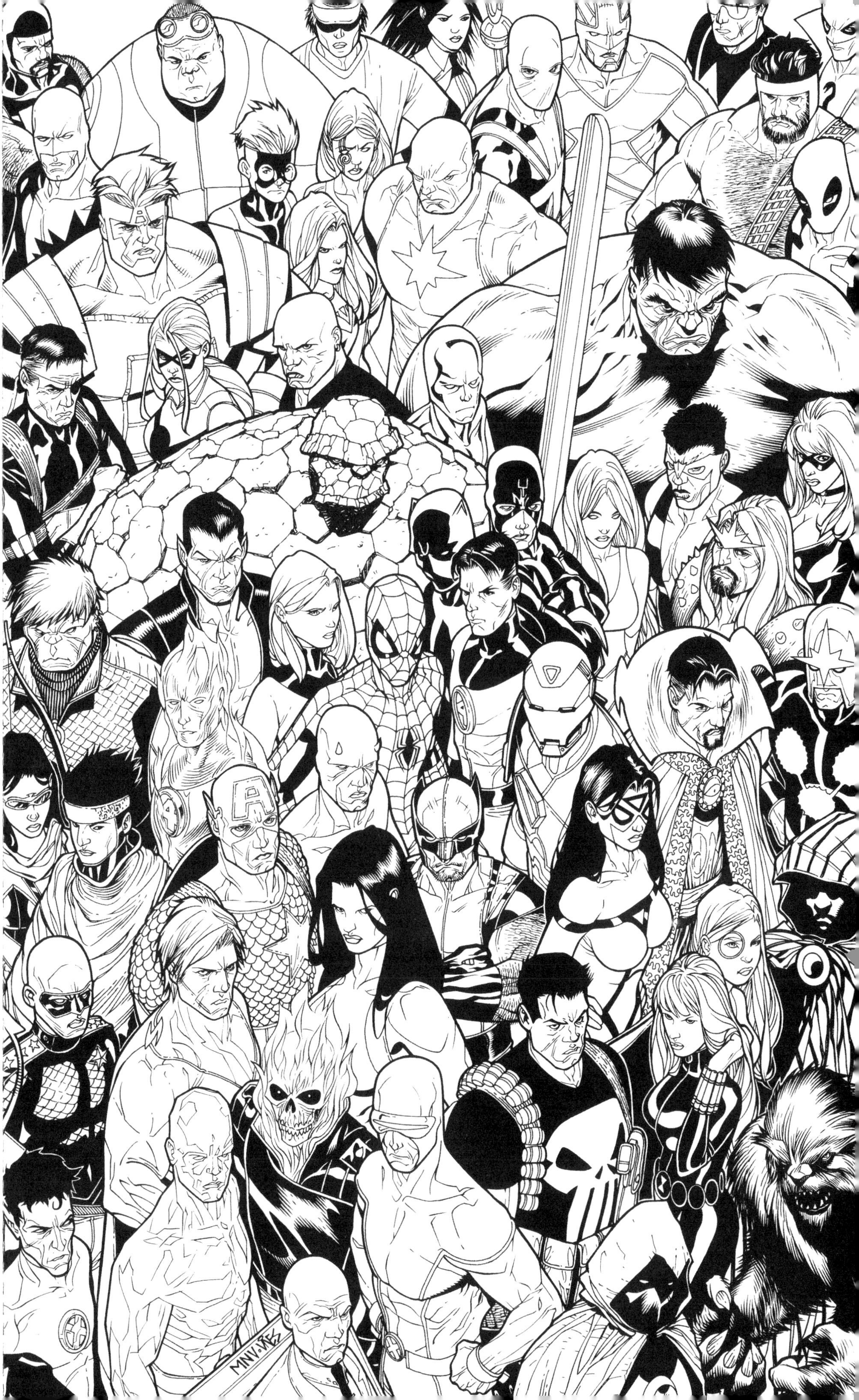

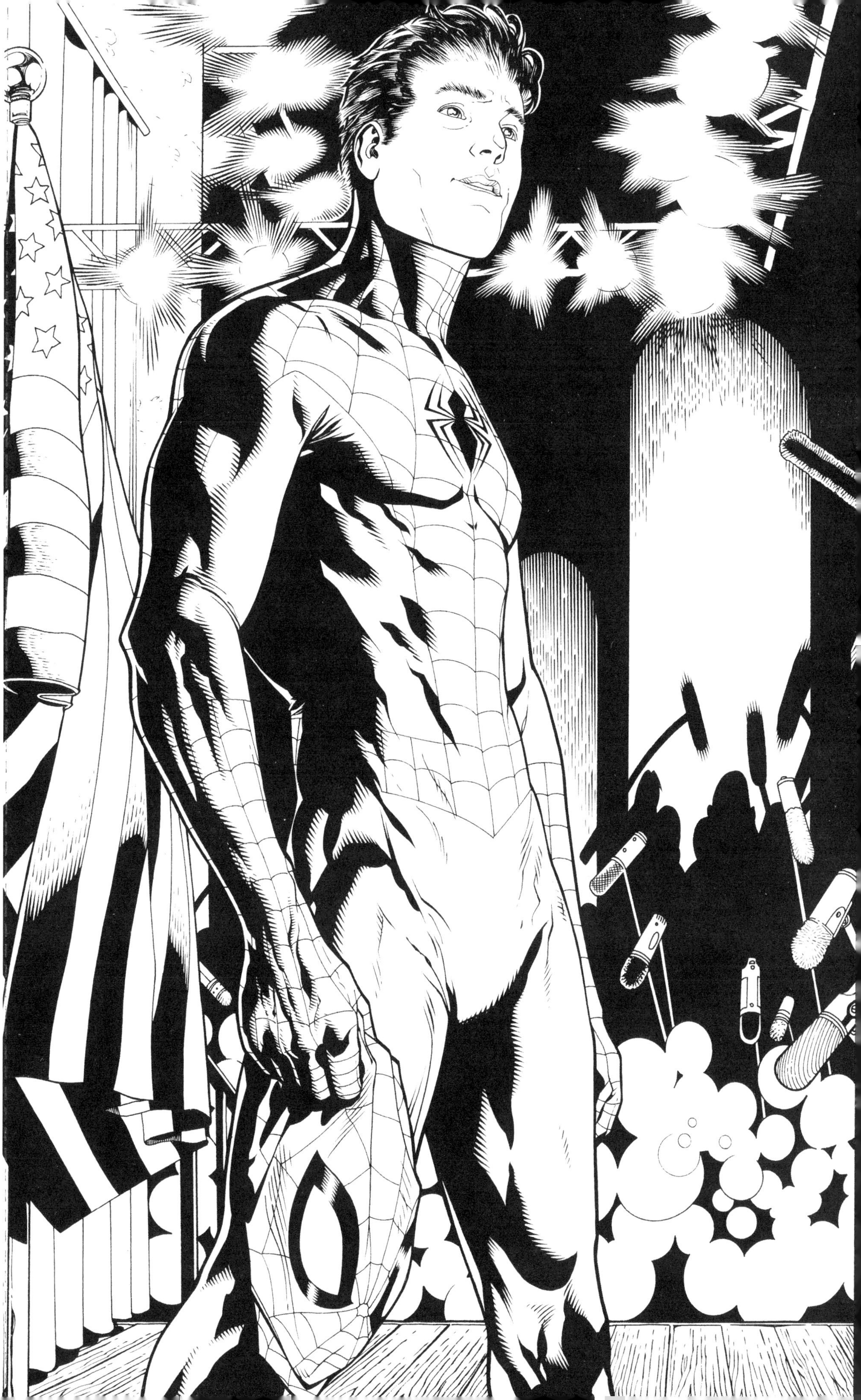

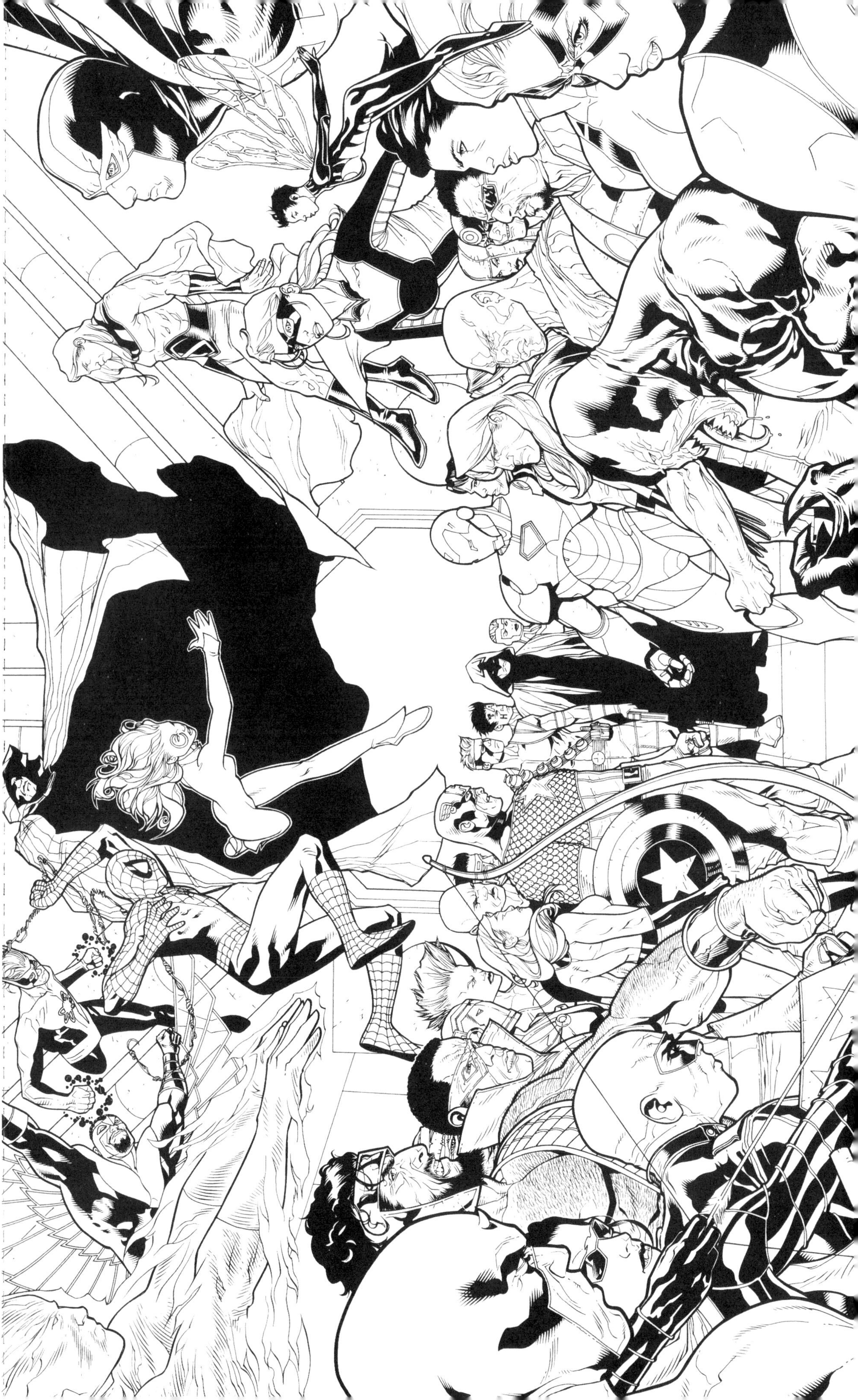

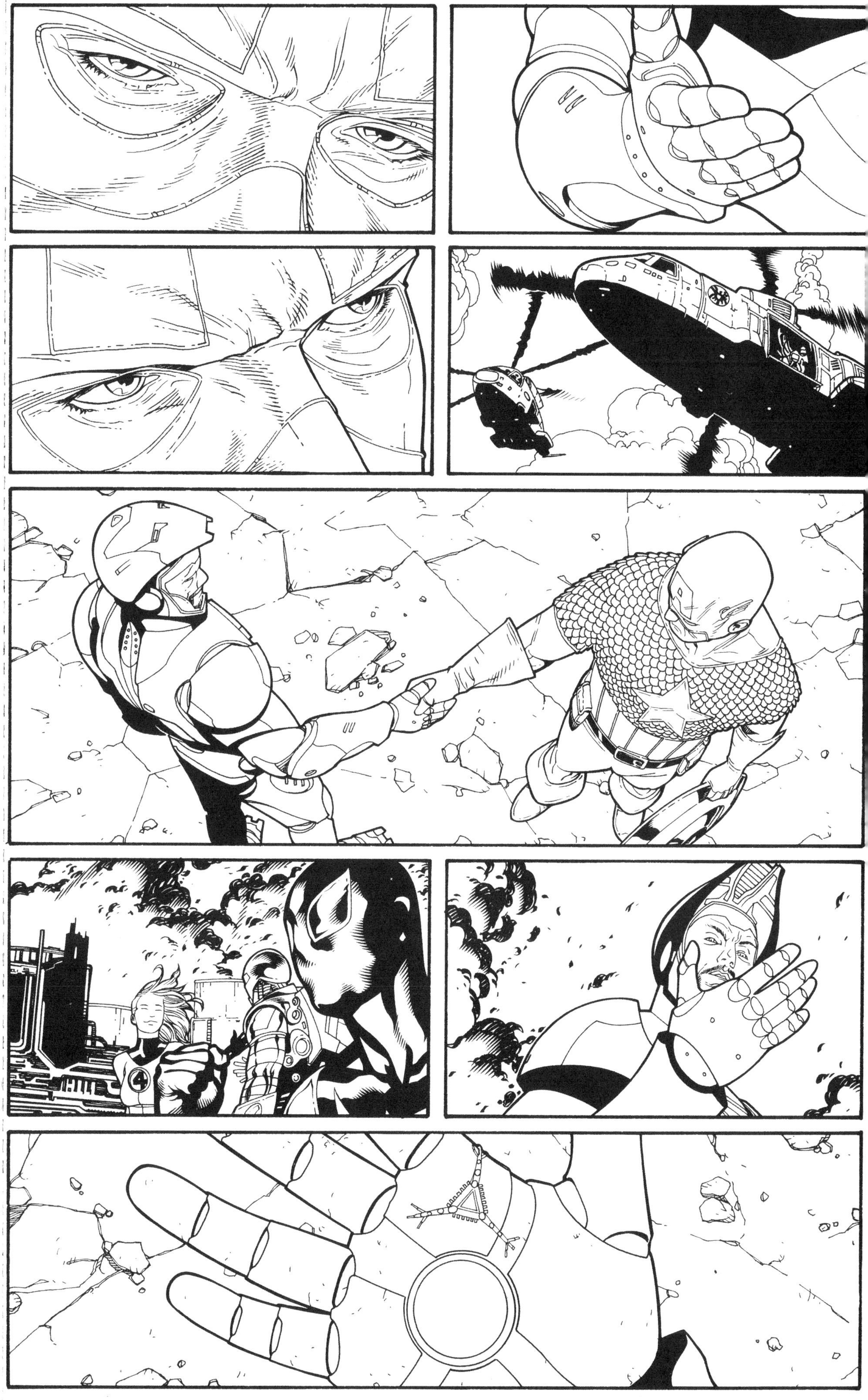

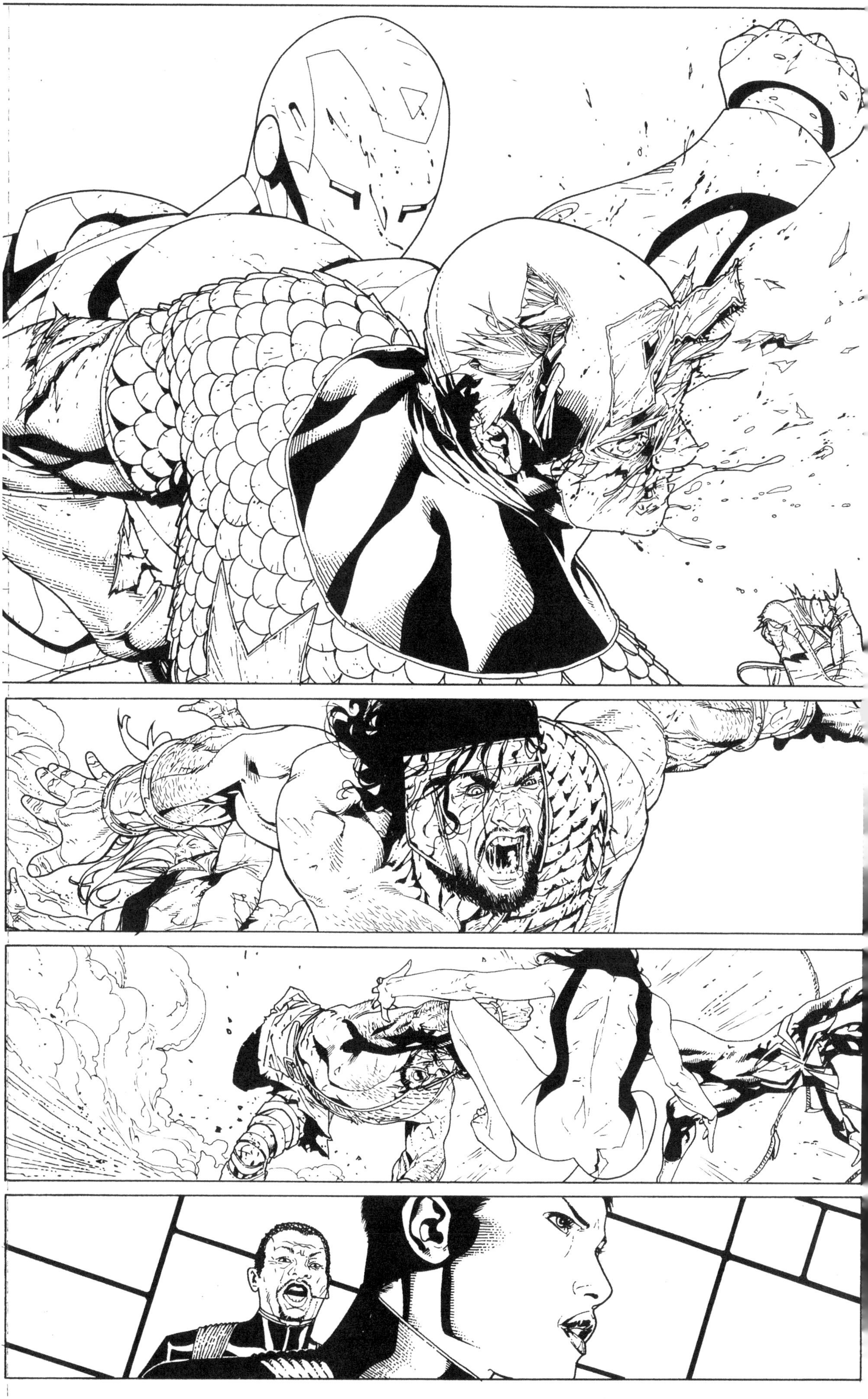

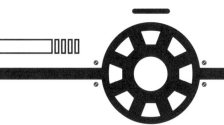

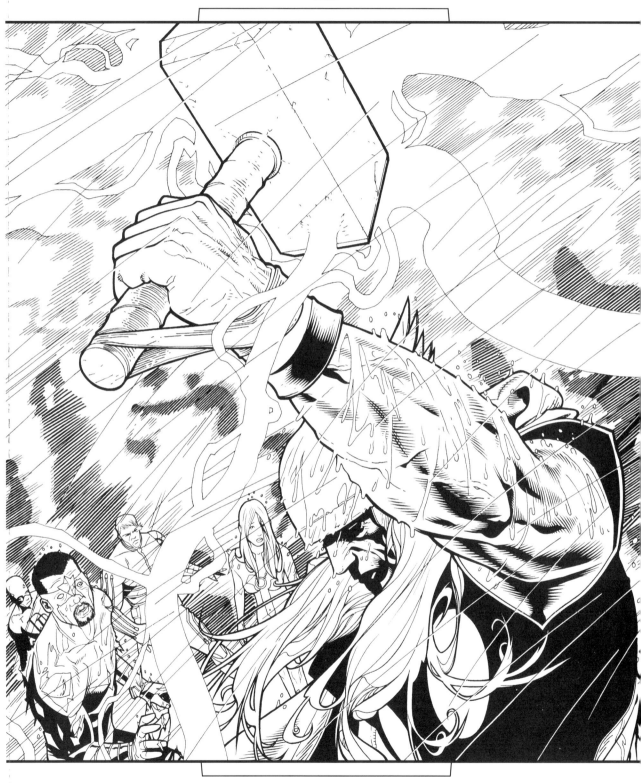

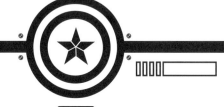

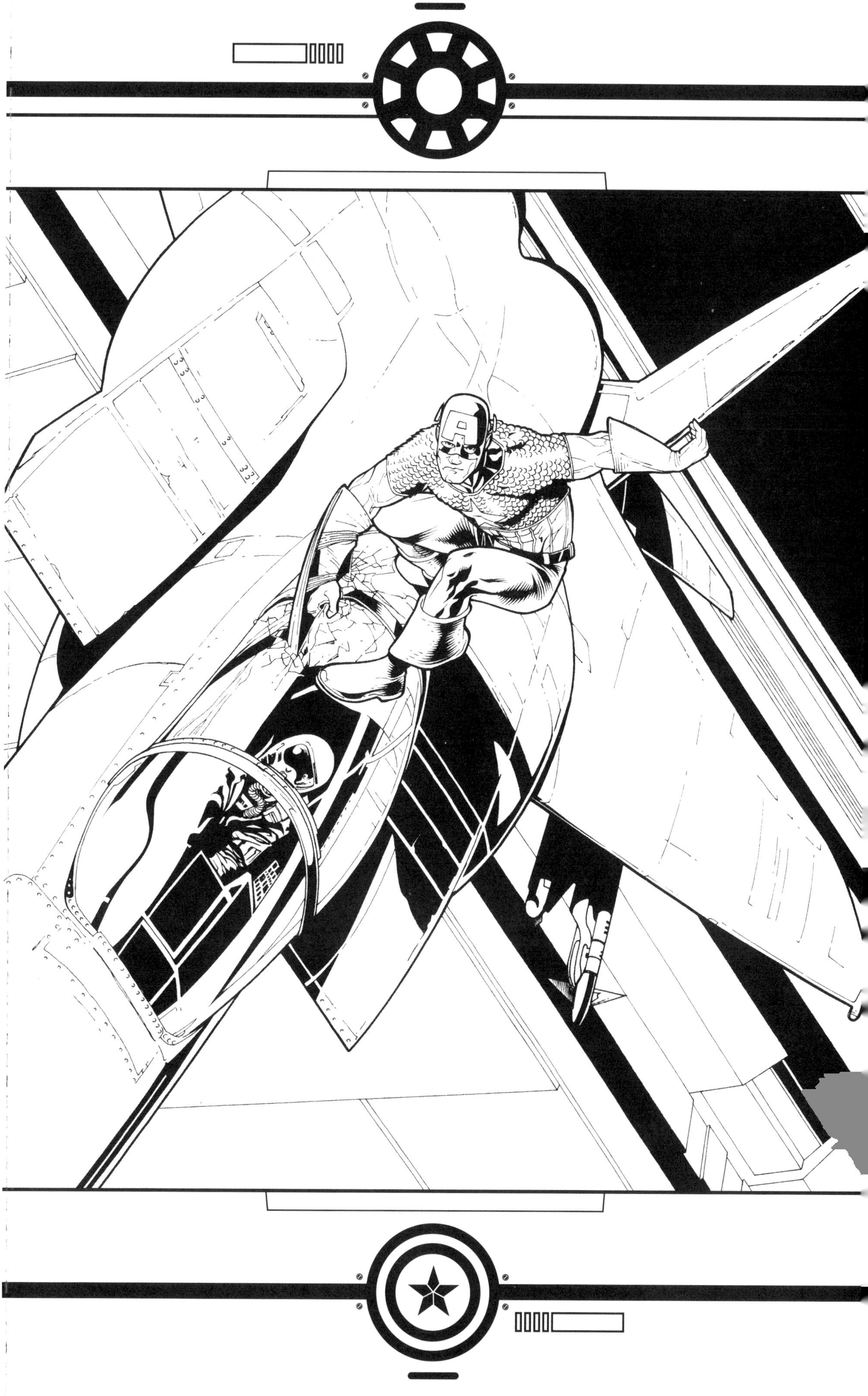

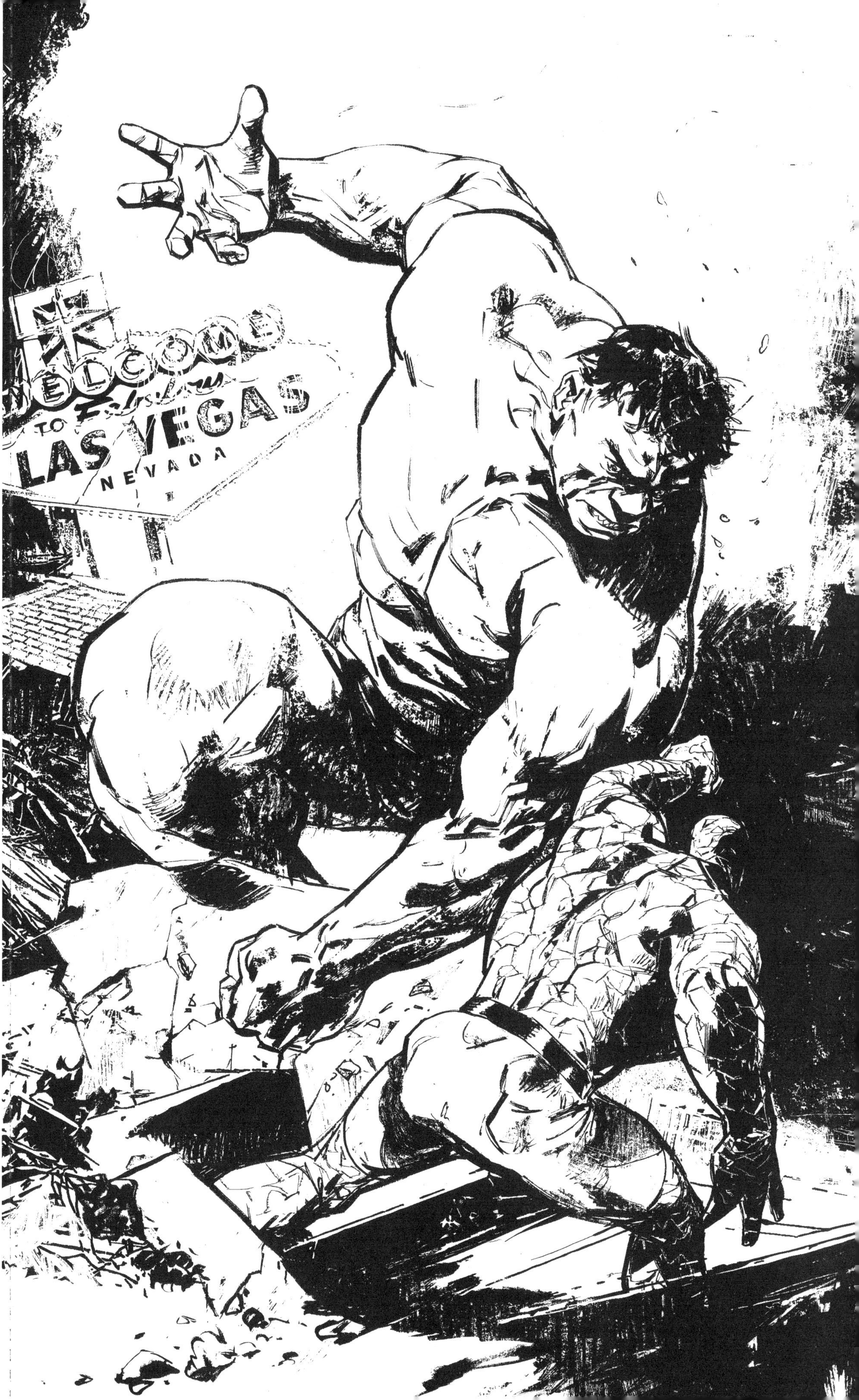
WELCOME
TO Fabulous
LAS VEGAS
NEVADA

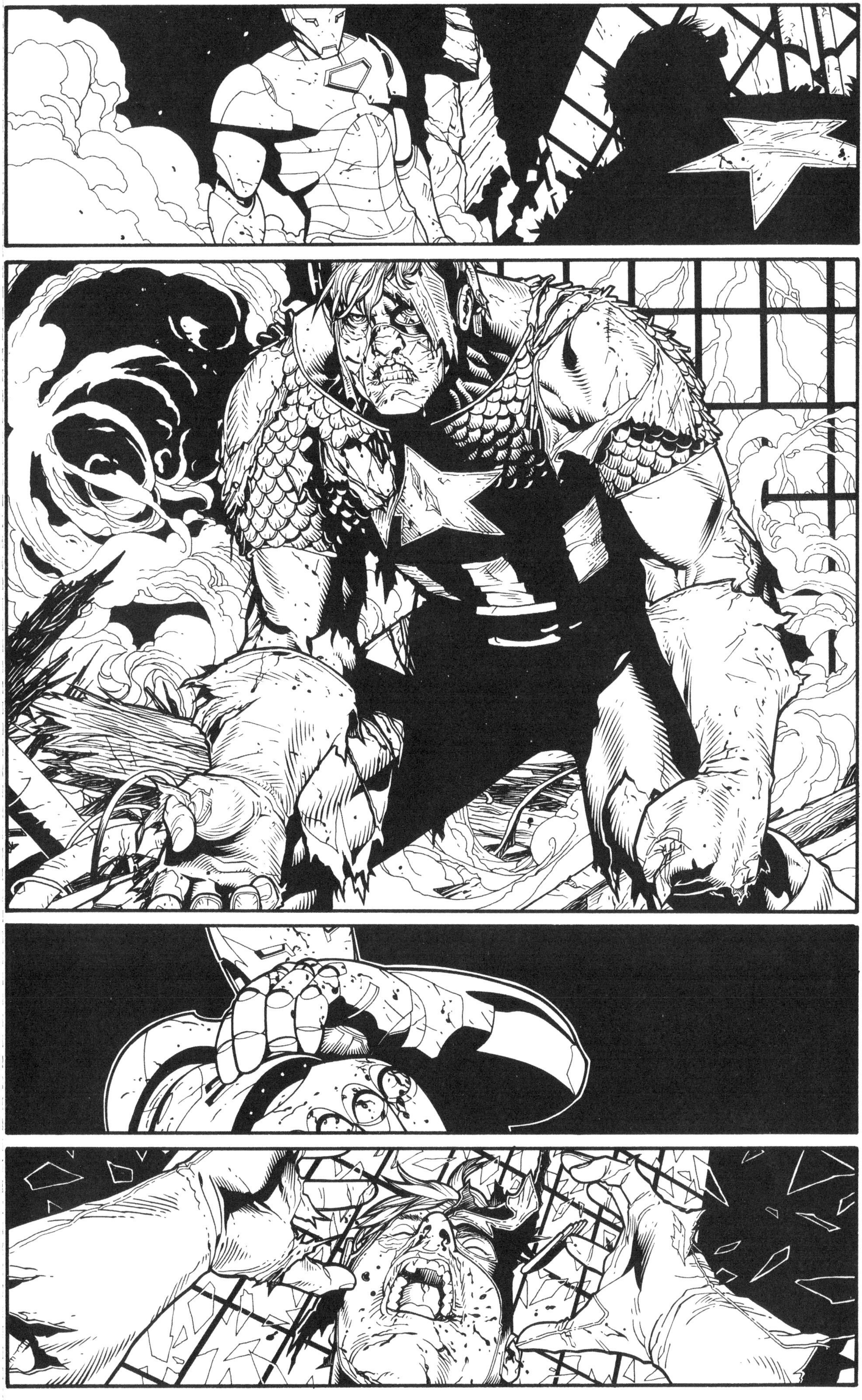

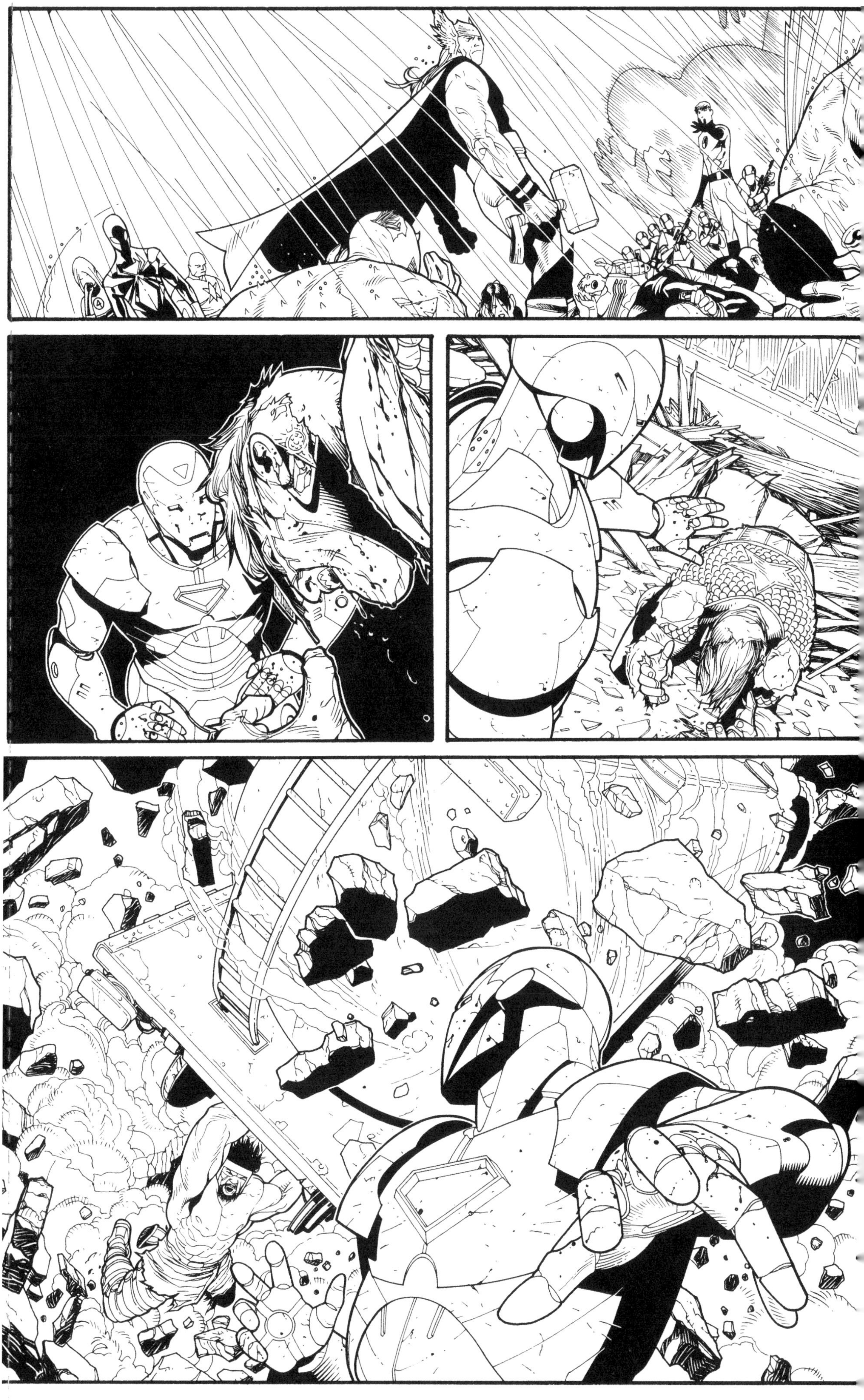

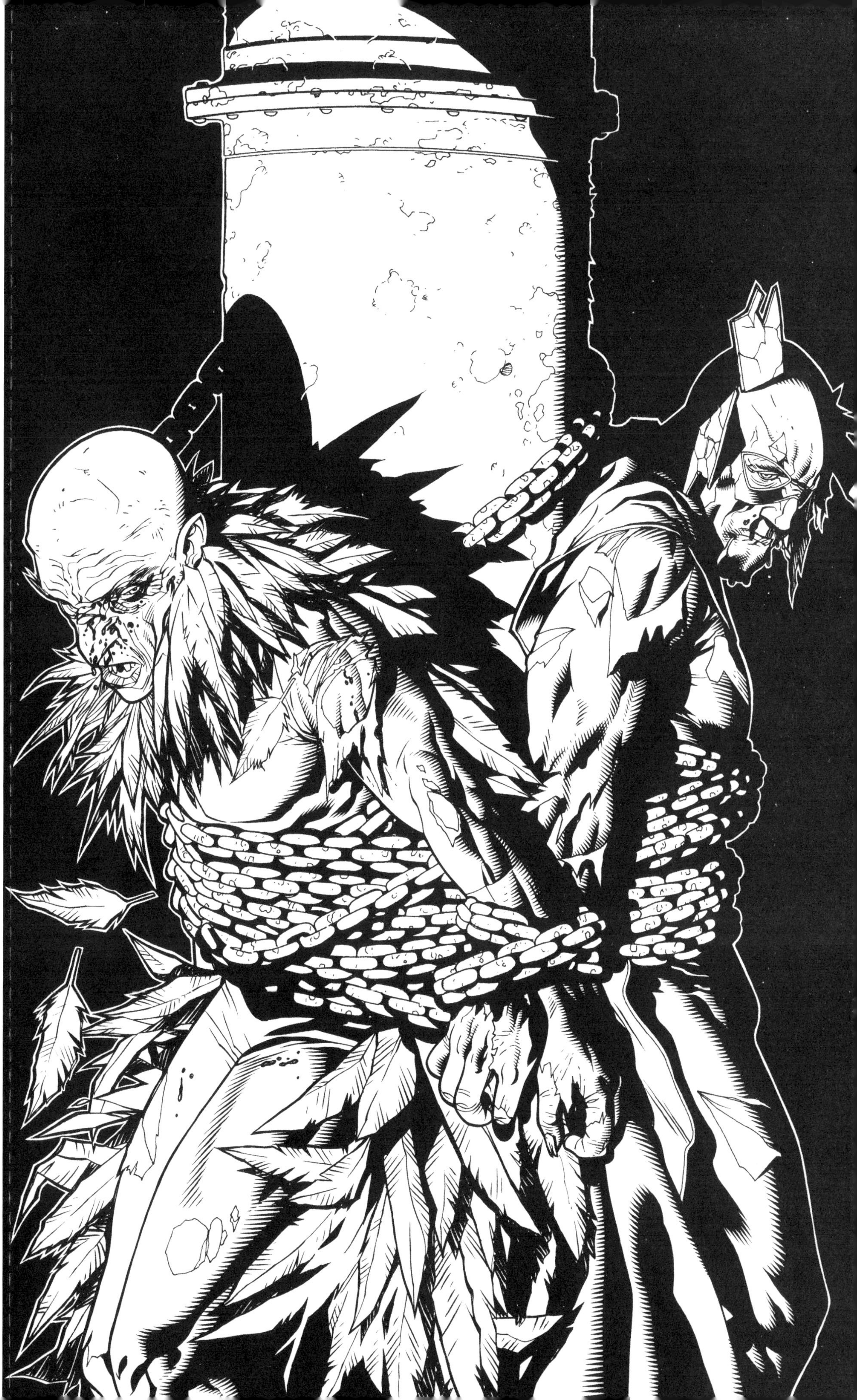

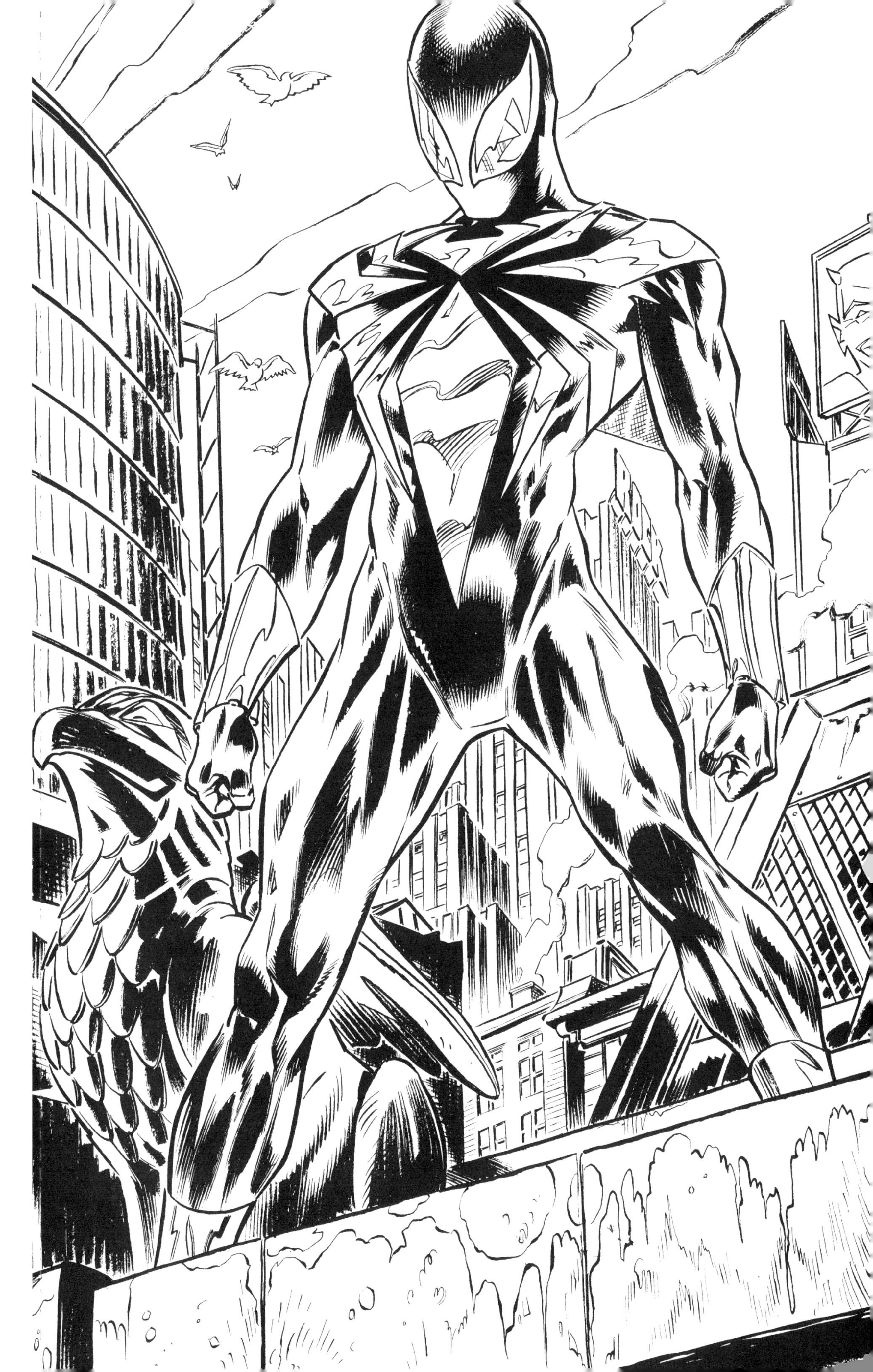

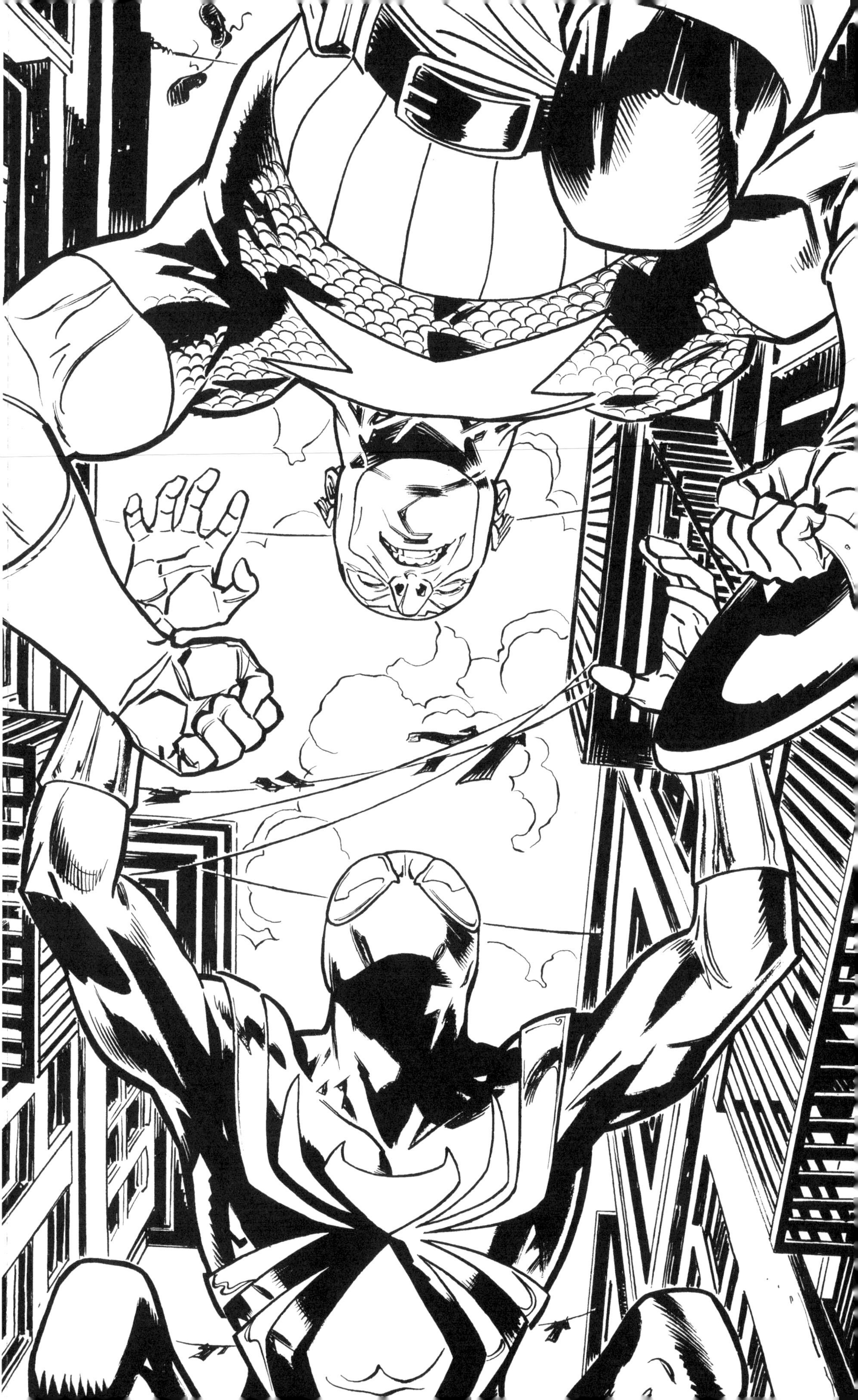

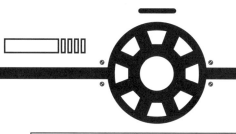

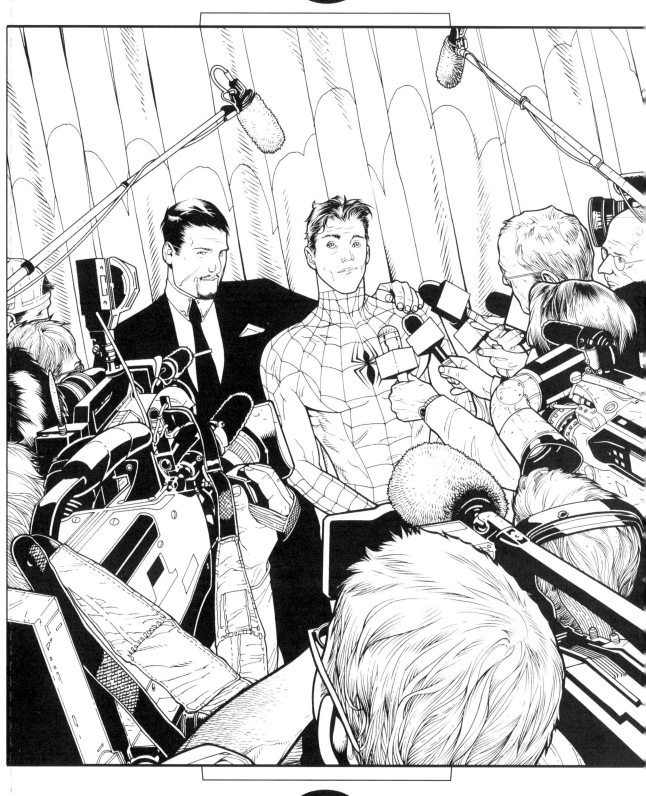

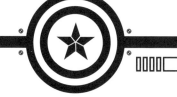

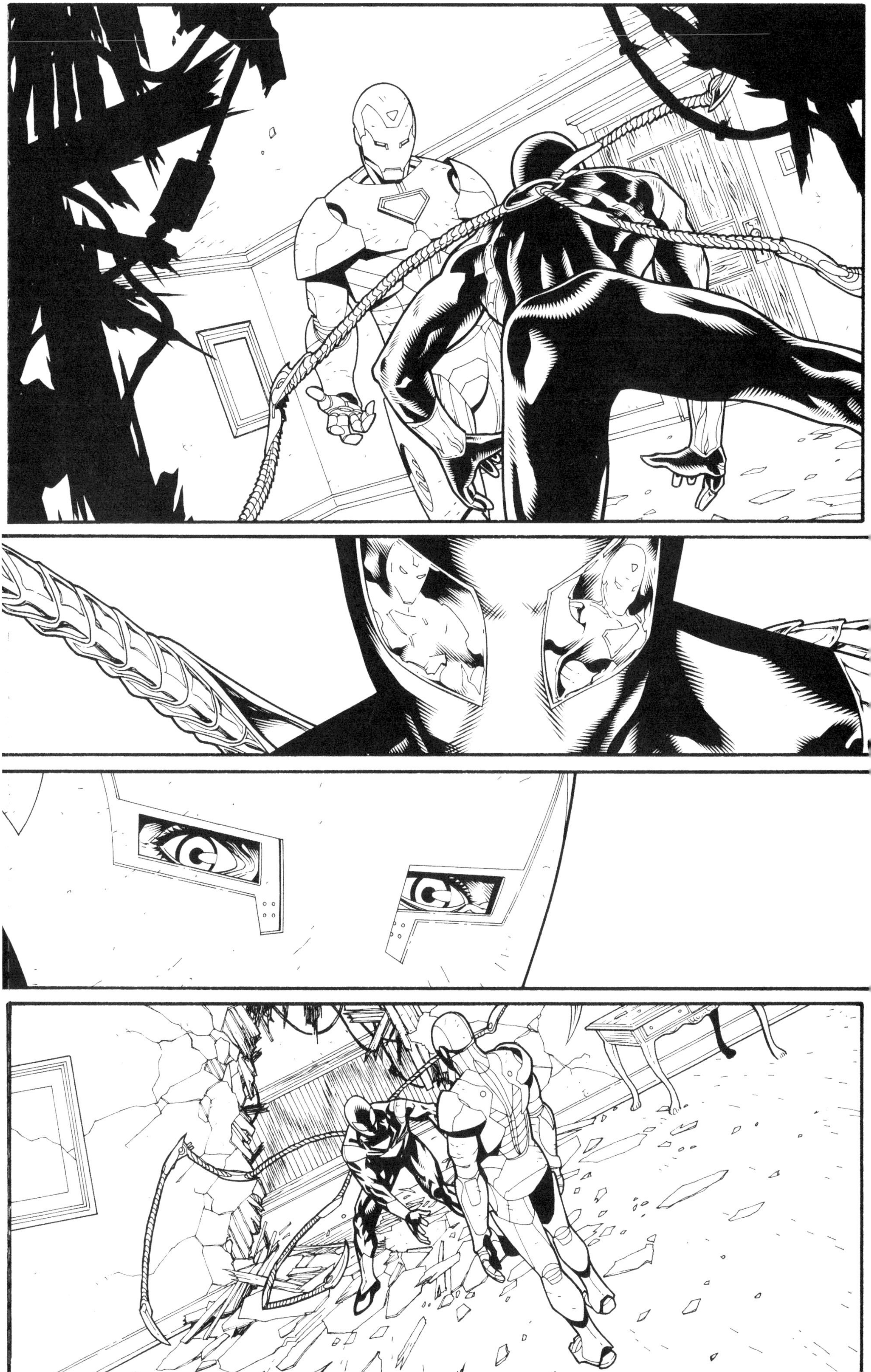

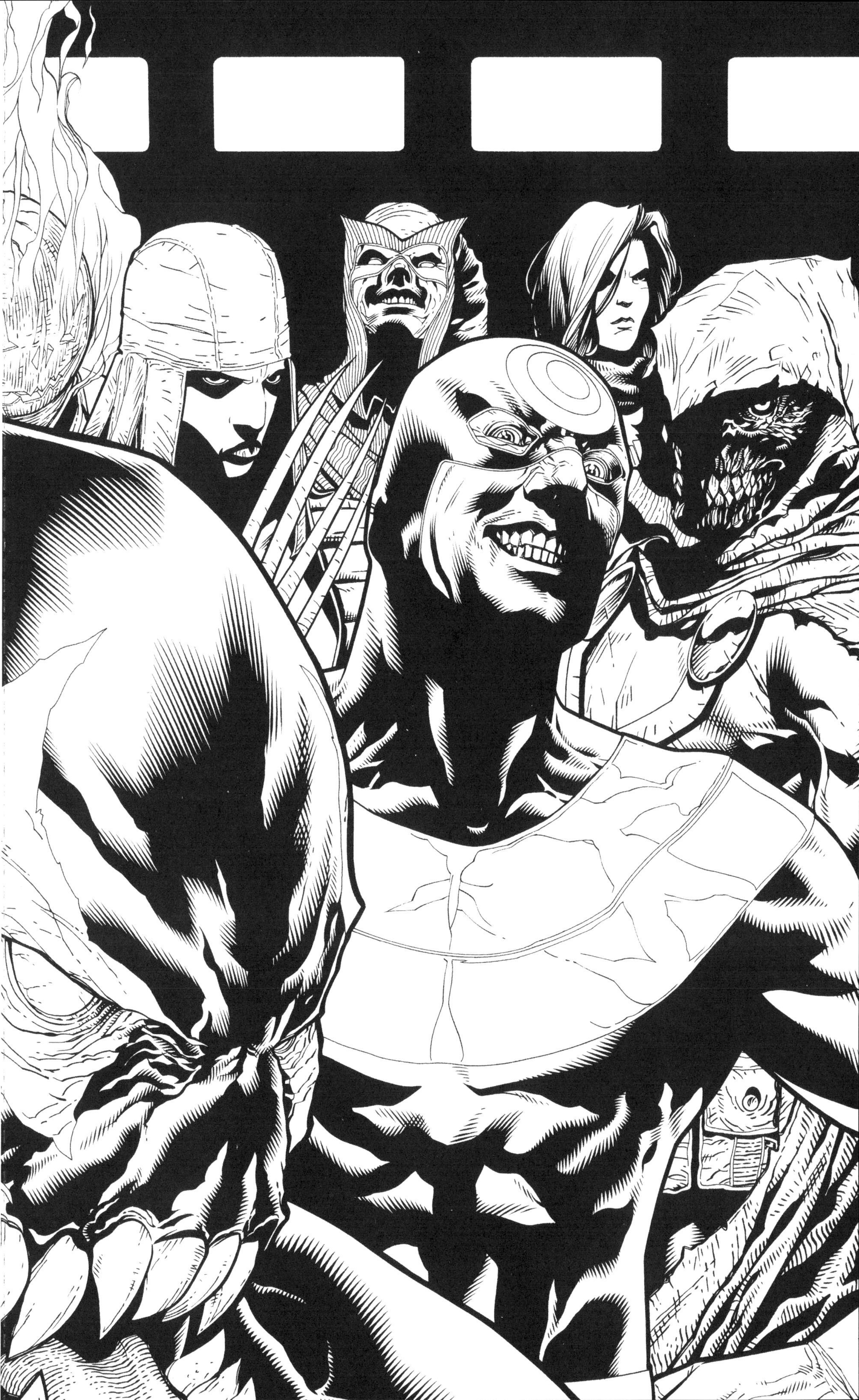

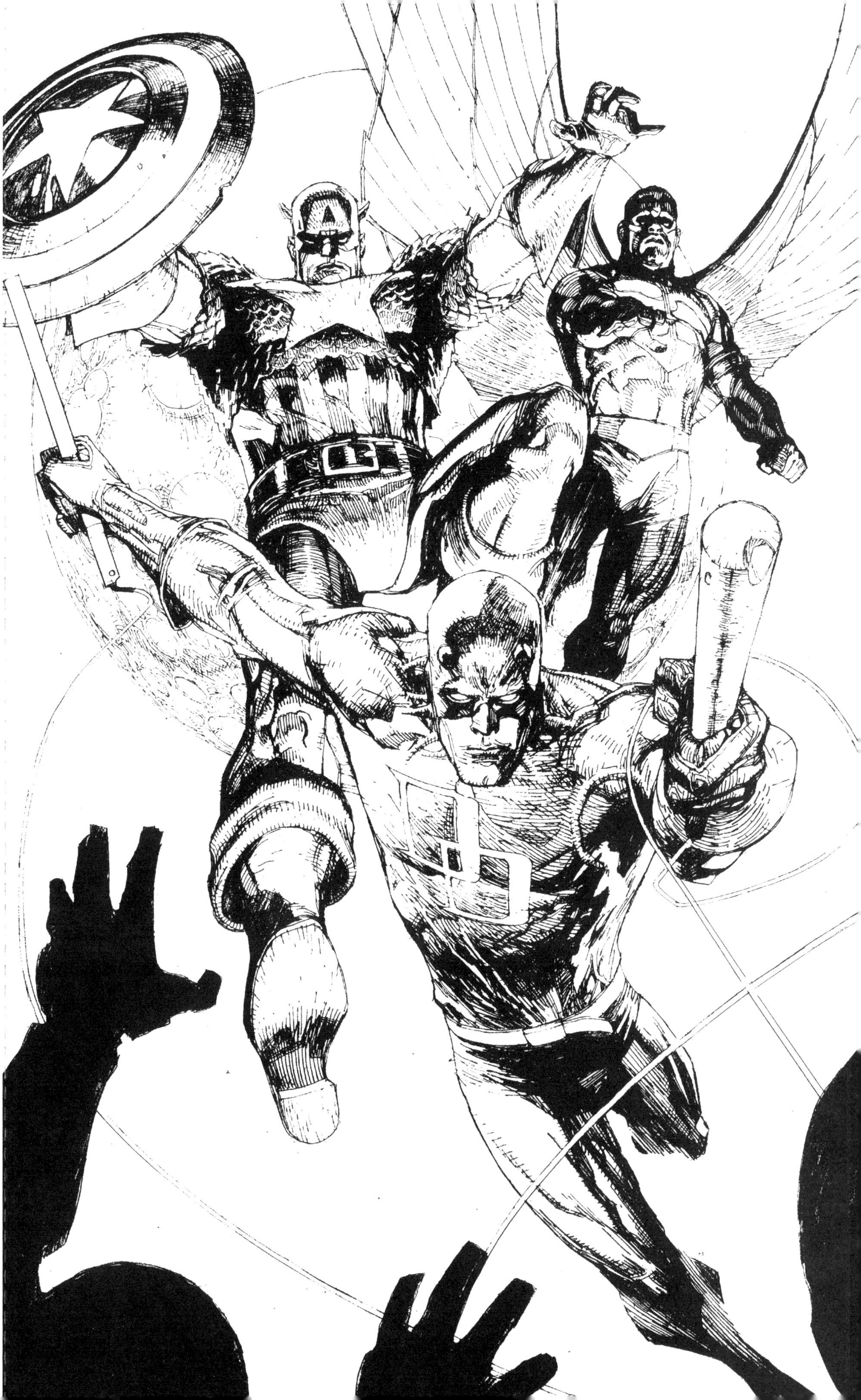

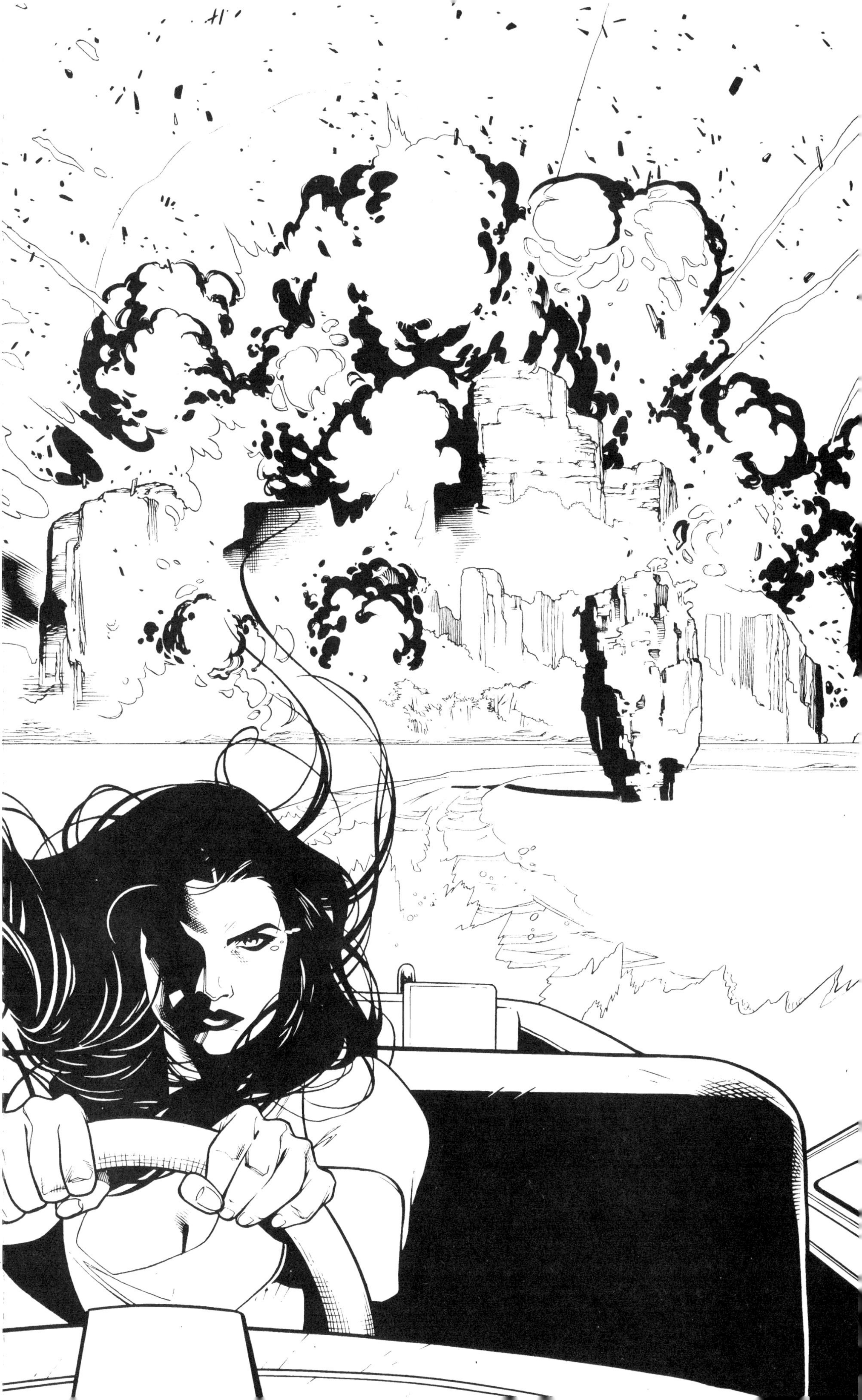

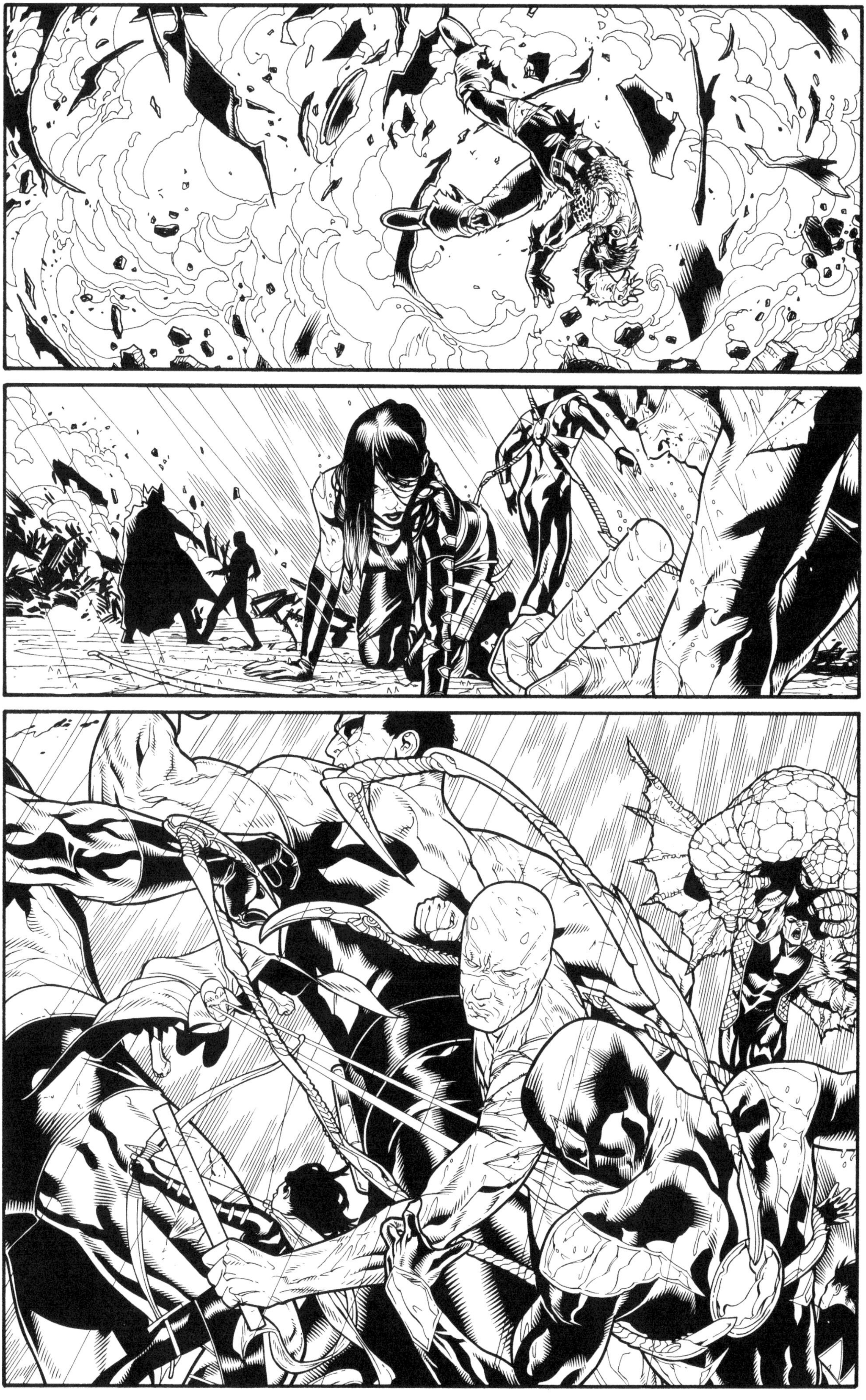

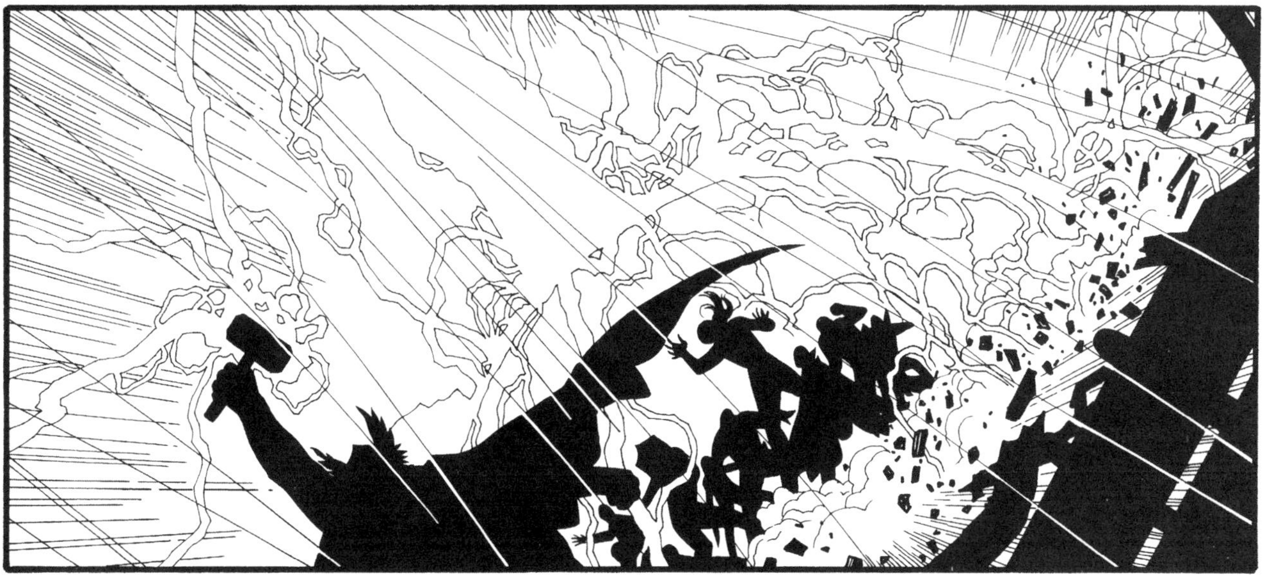

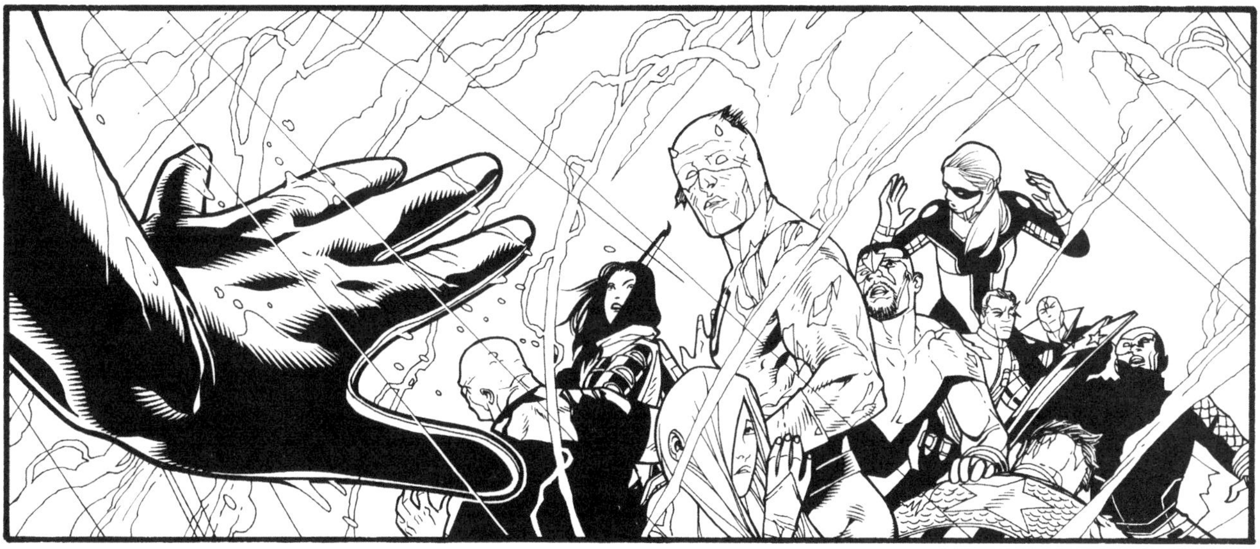

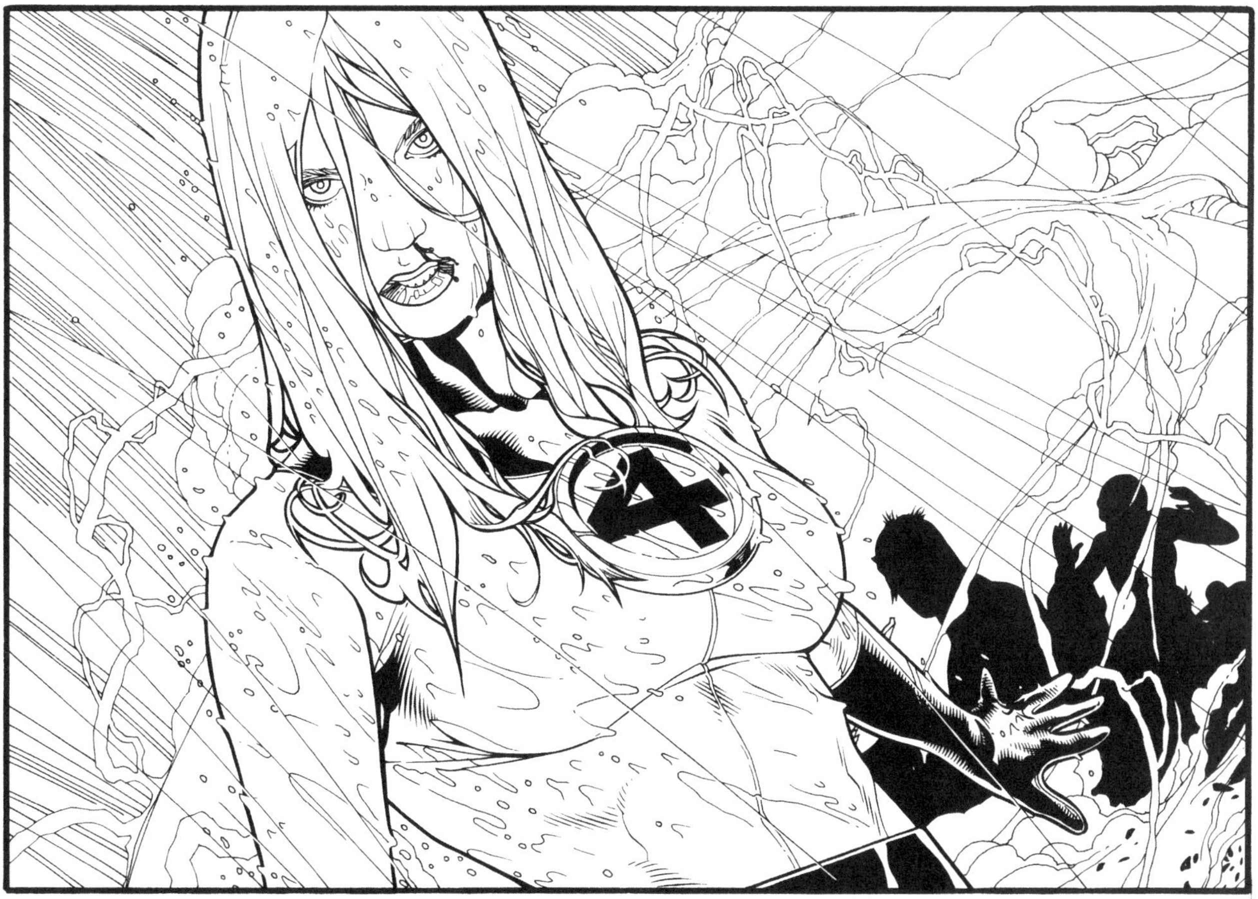

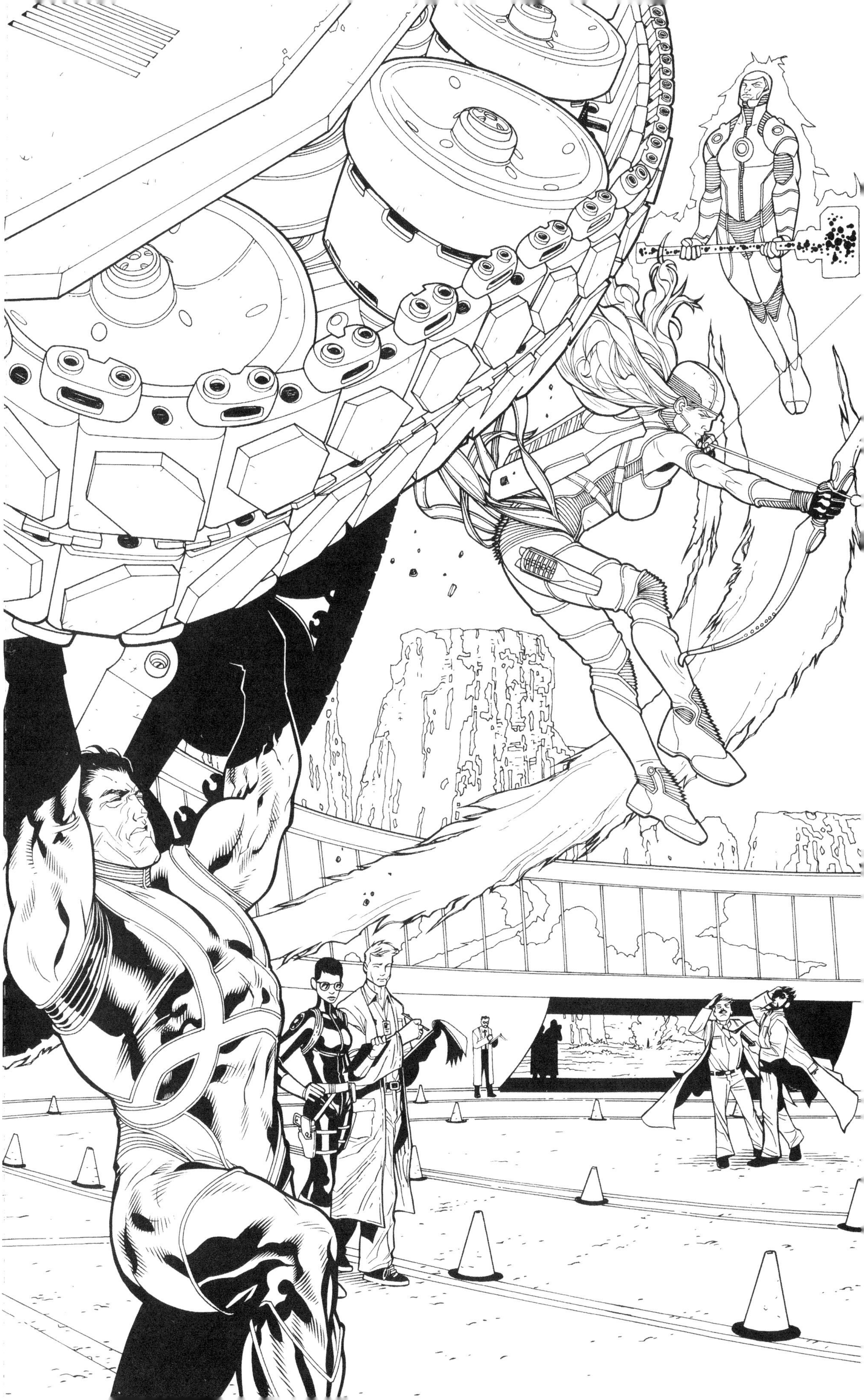

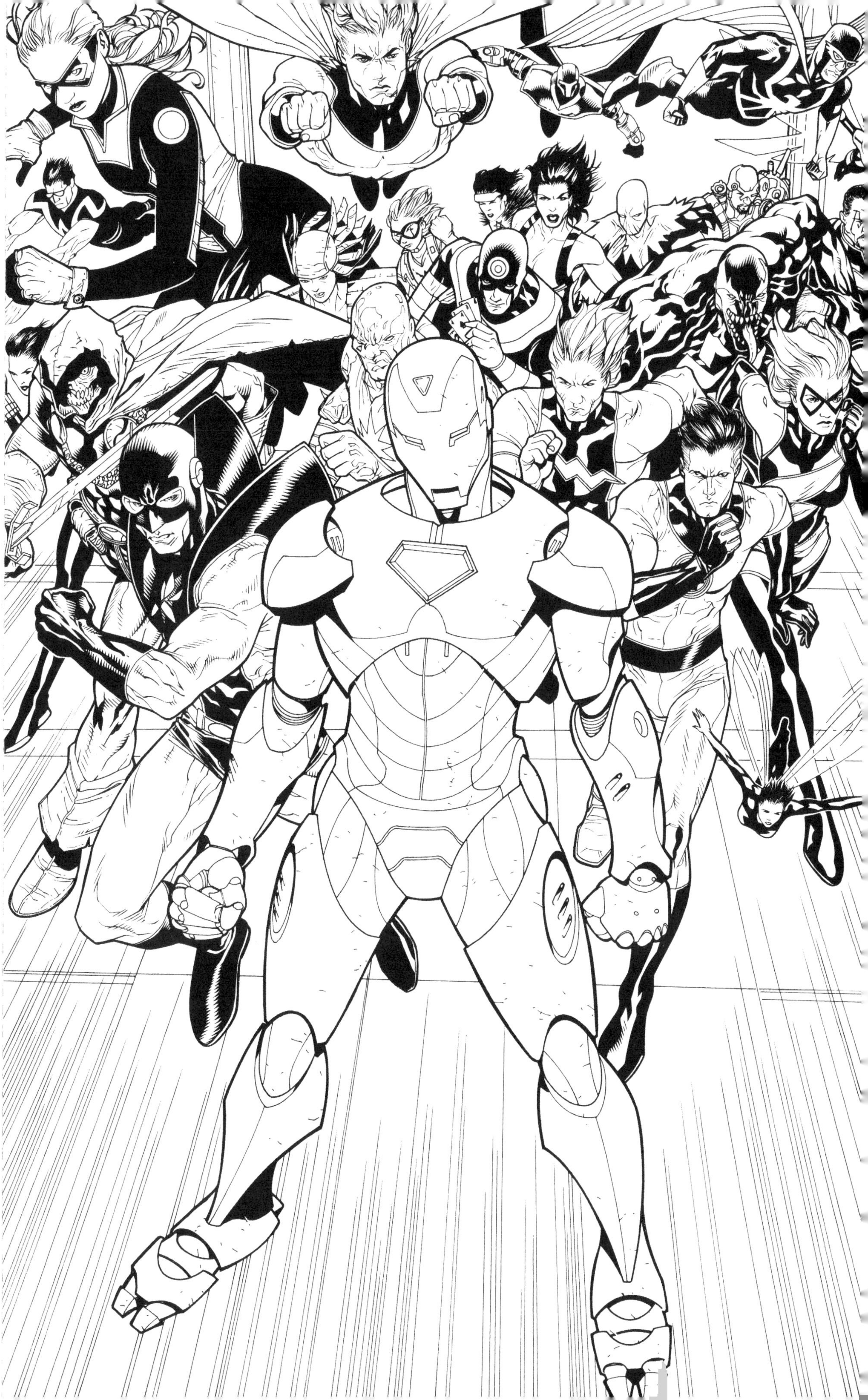

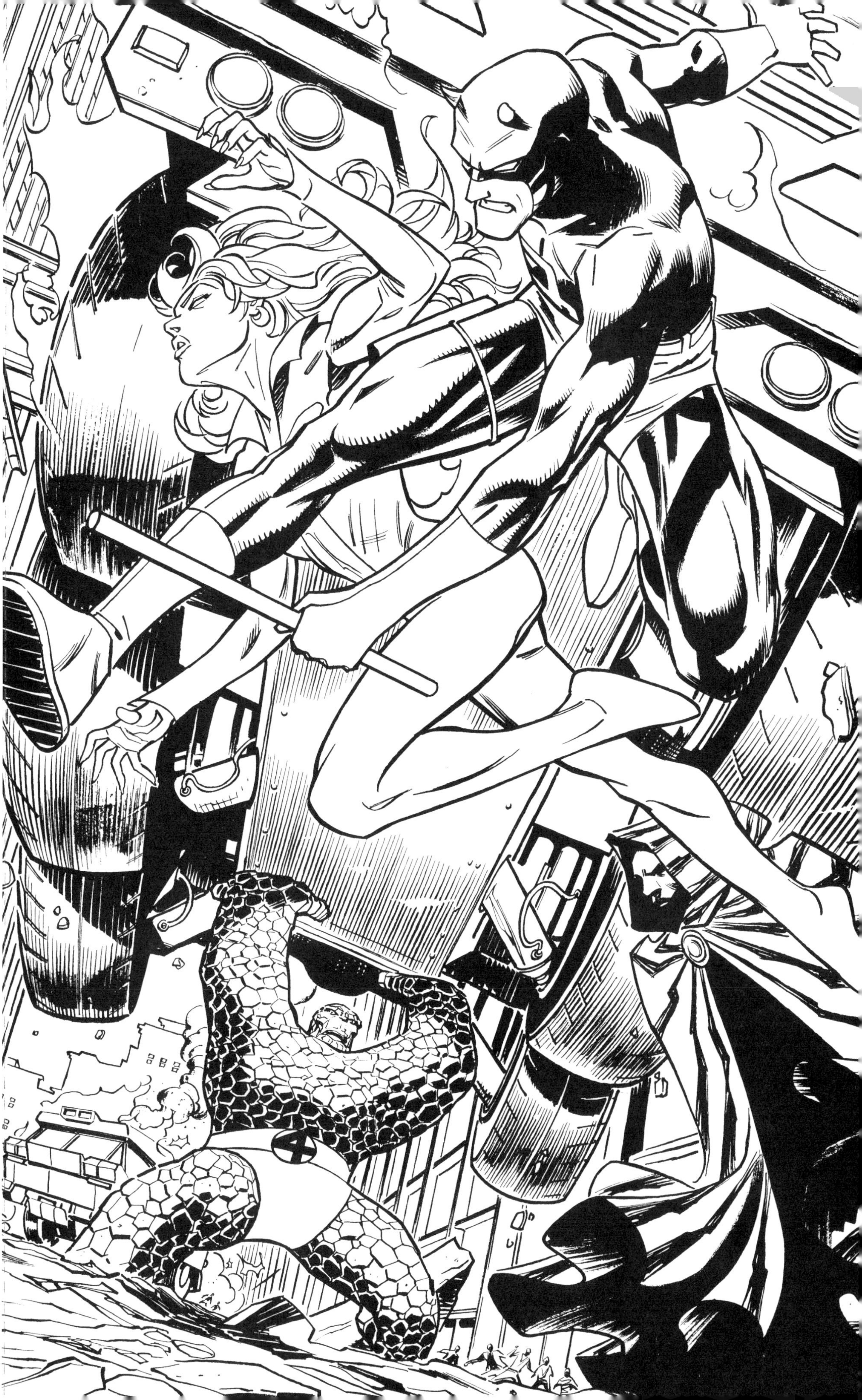

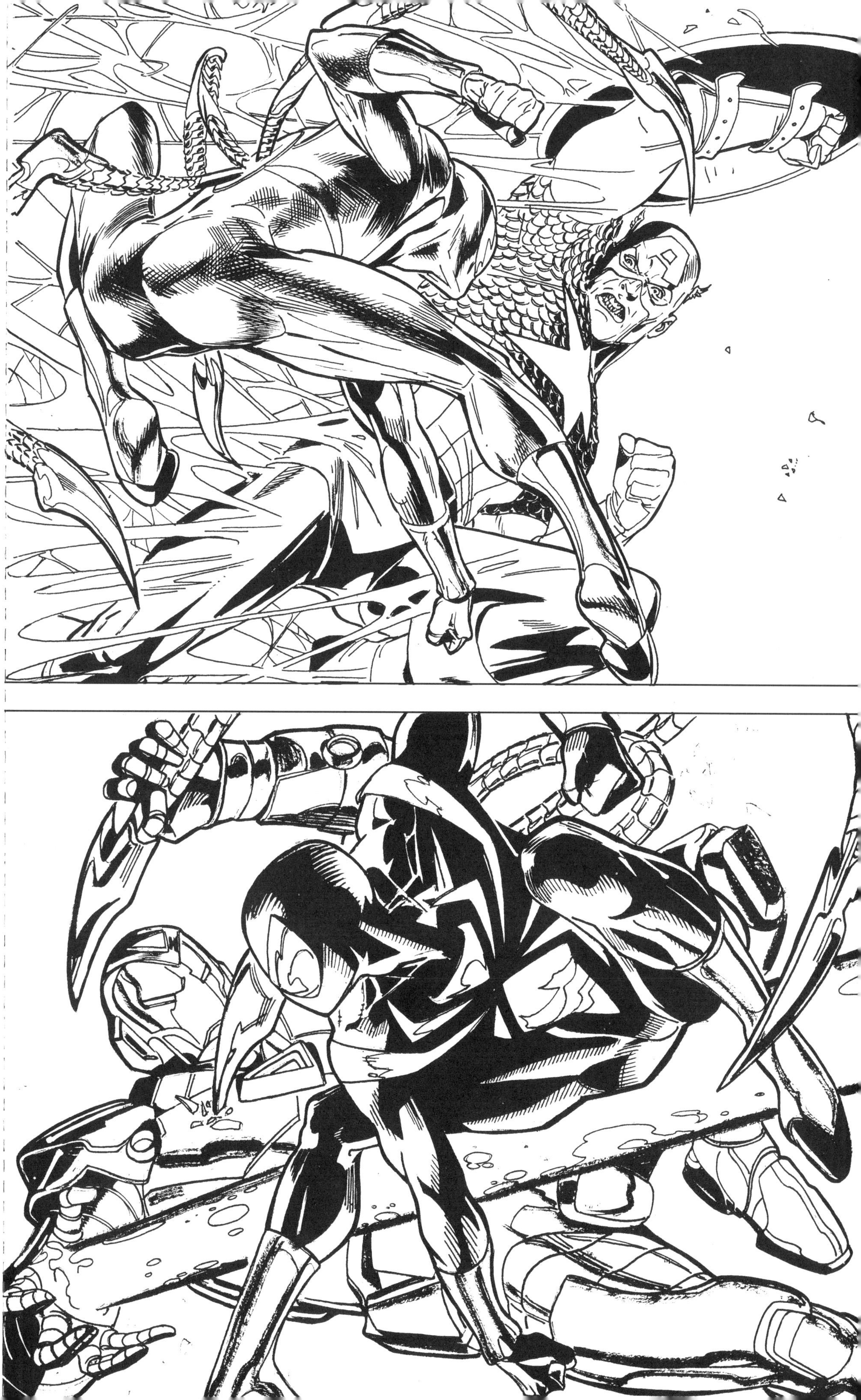

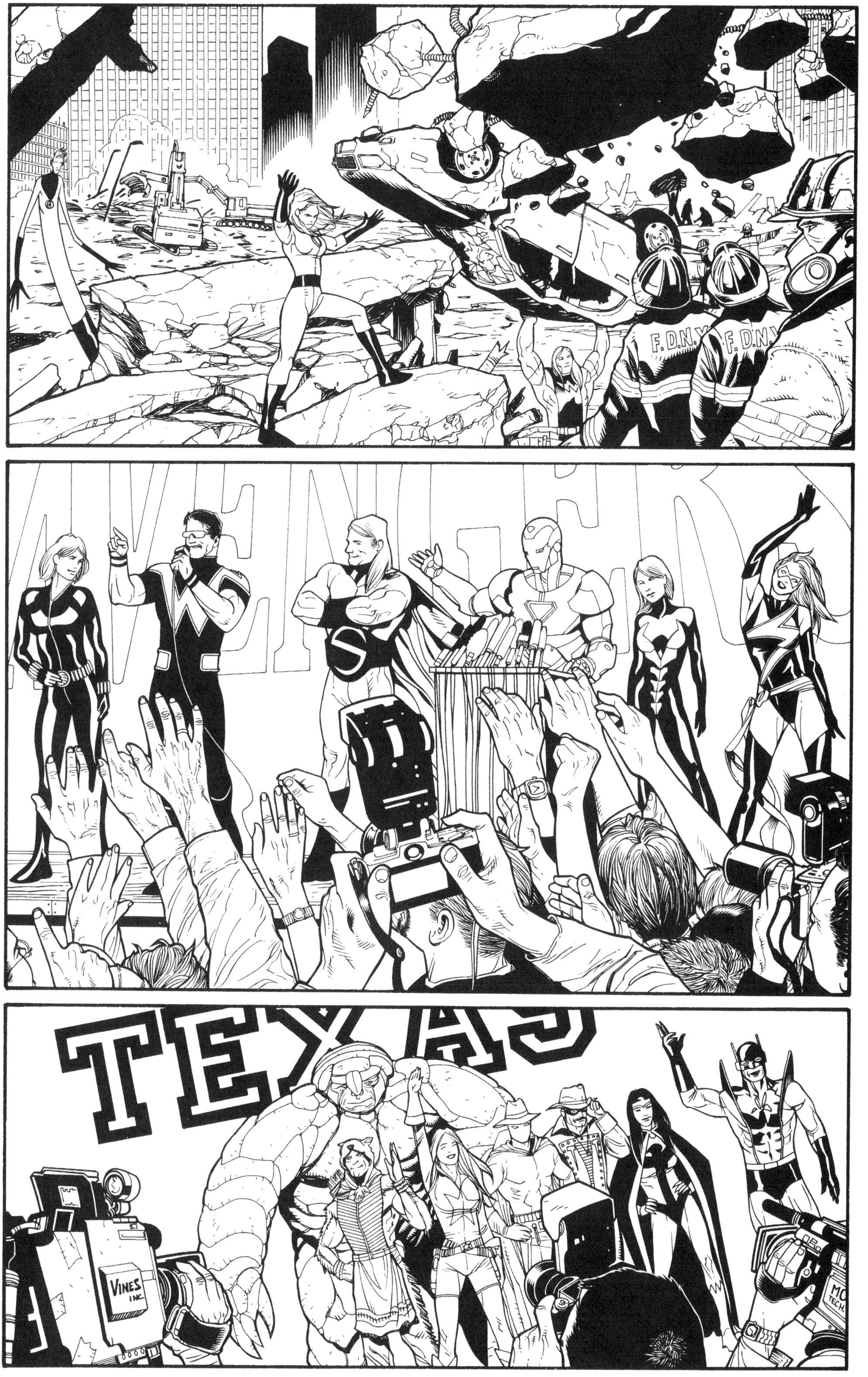
F.D.N.Y.
F.D.N.Y.
TEXAS
VINES INC.

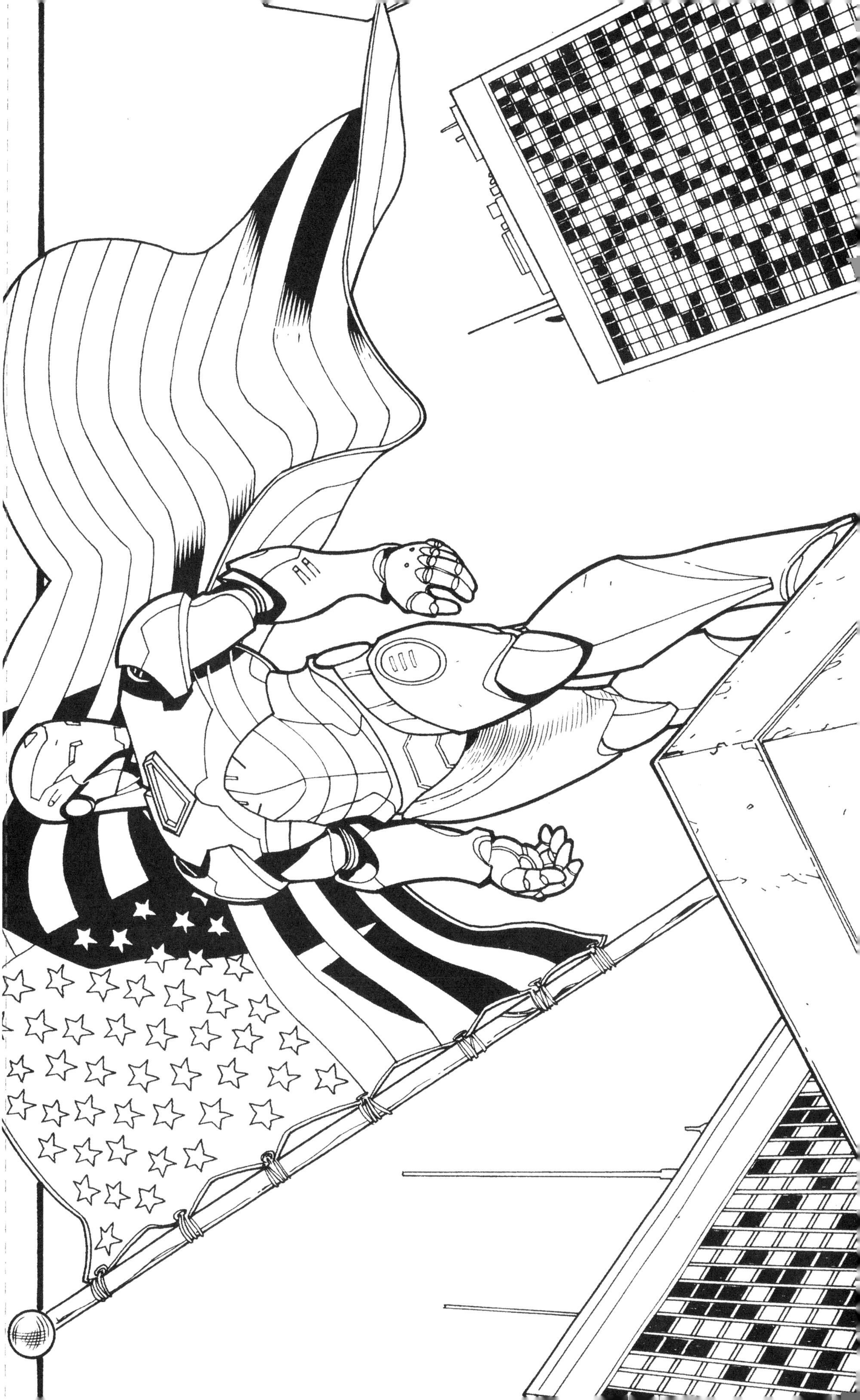

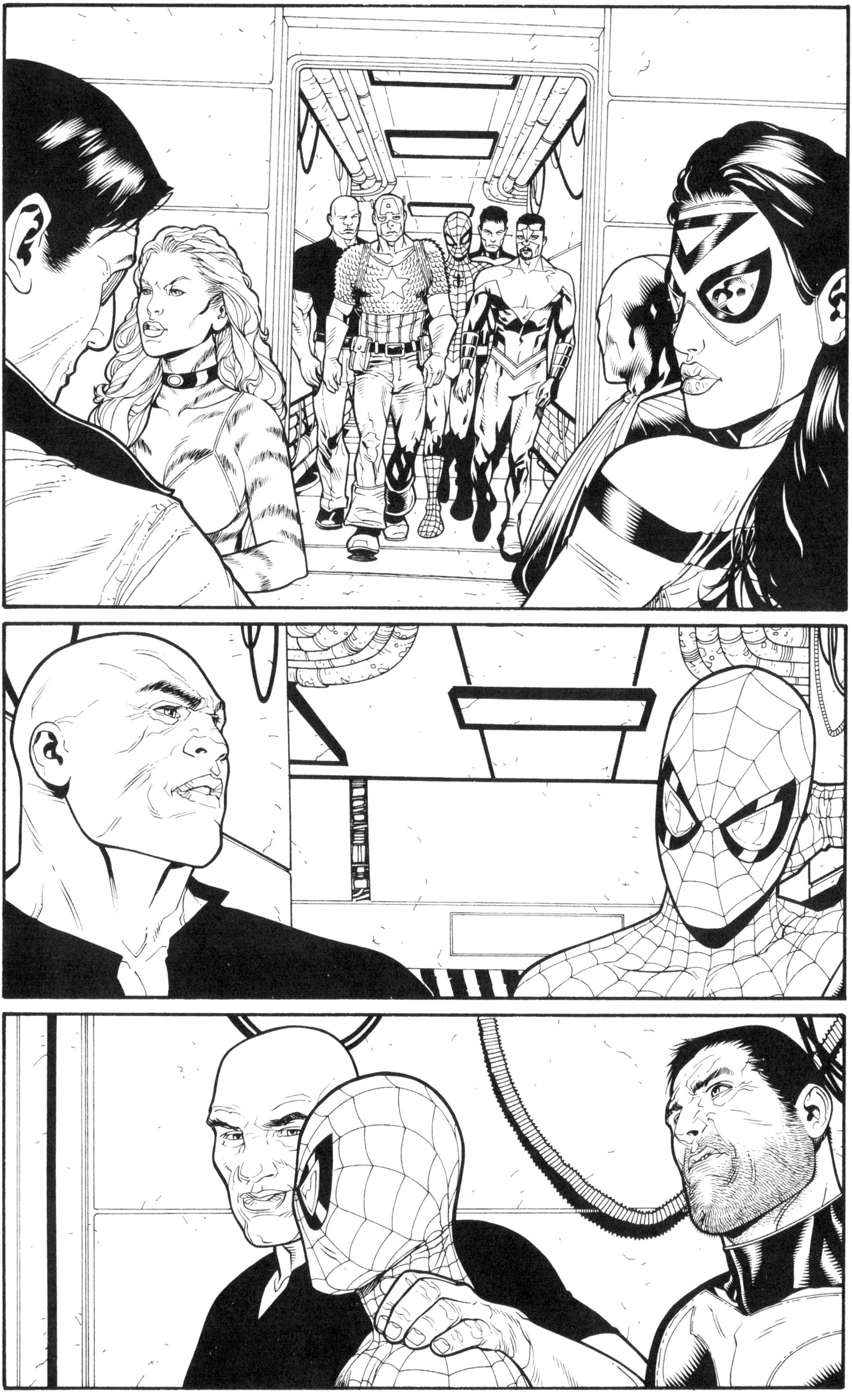

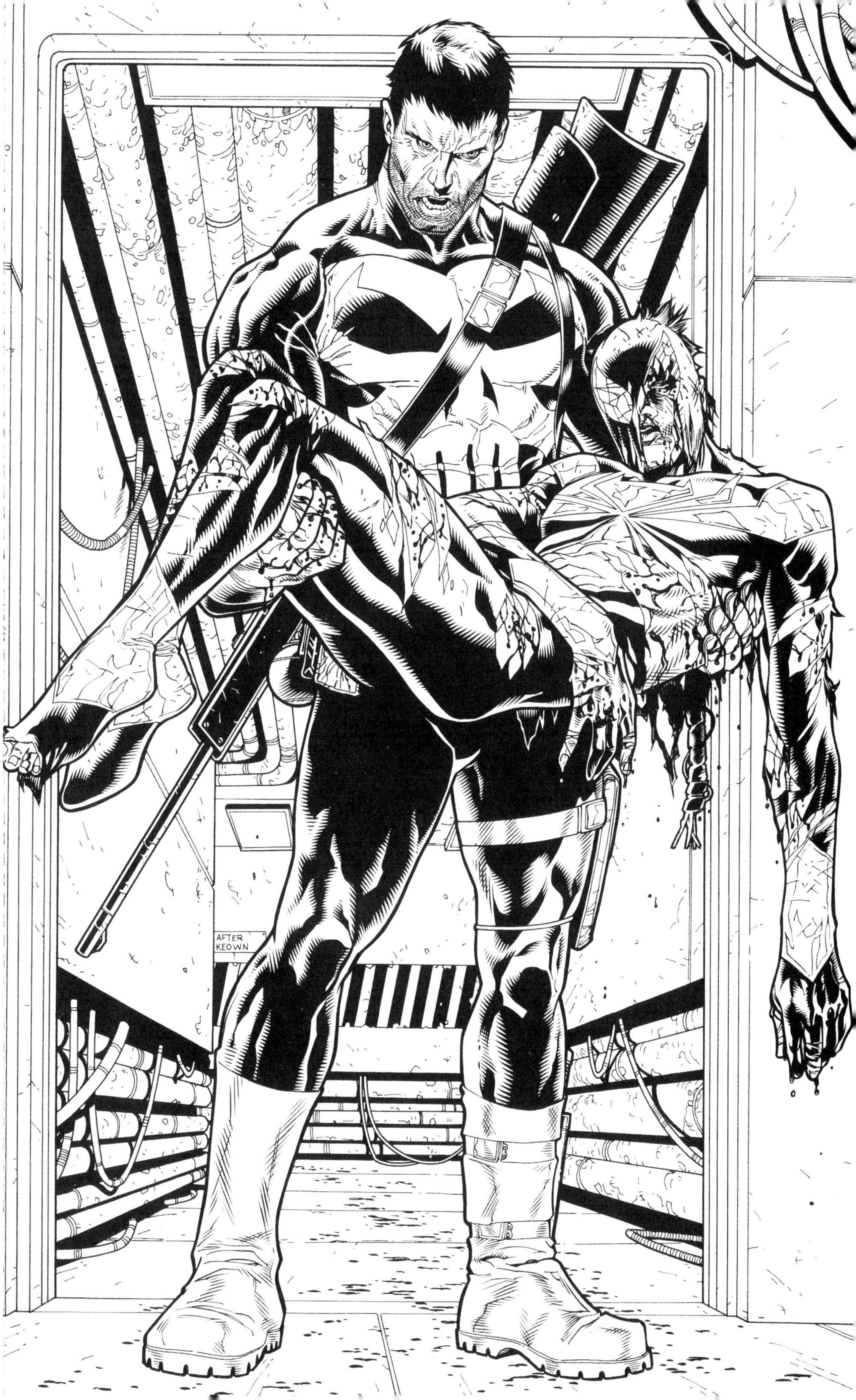
AFTER
KEOWN

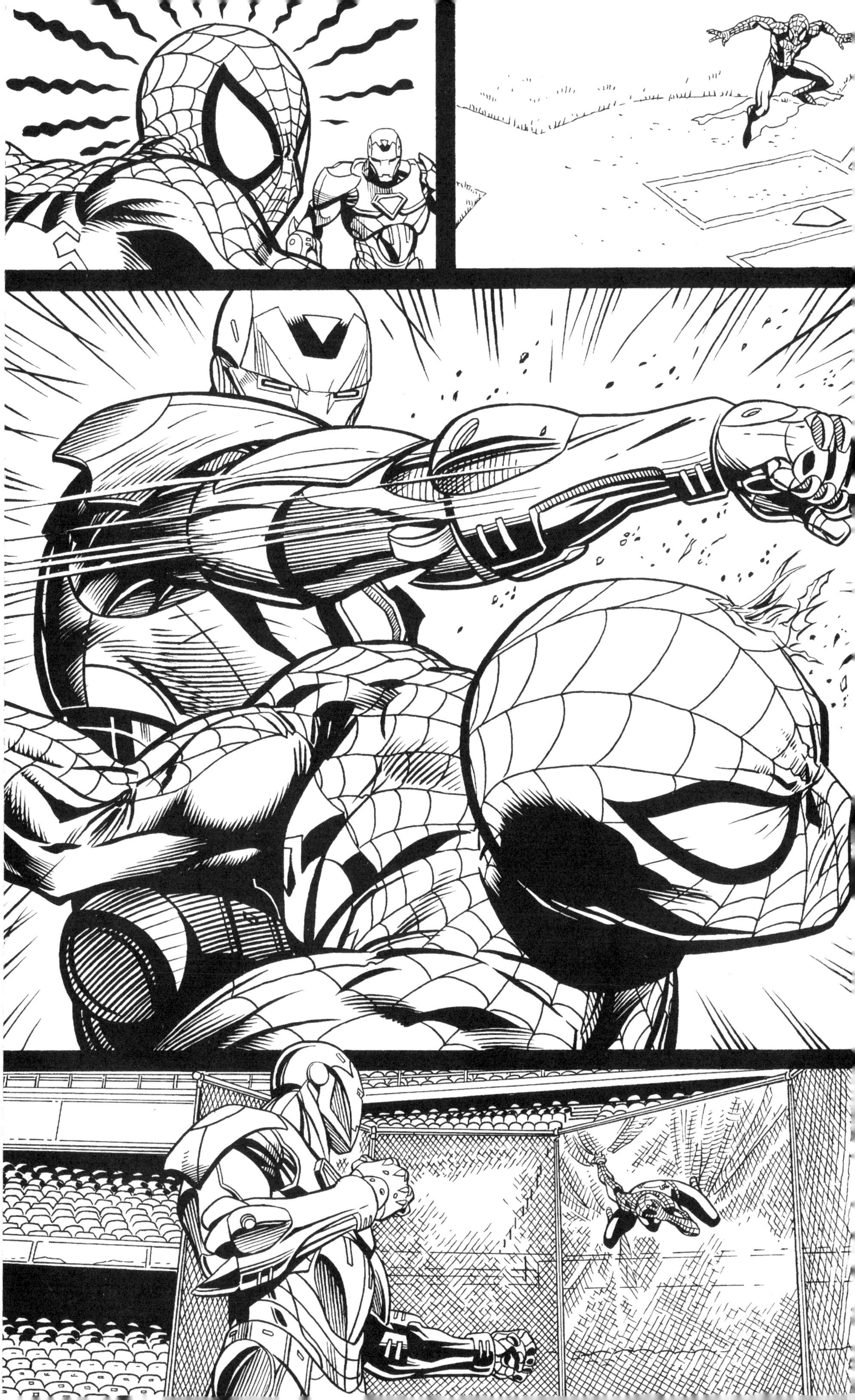

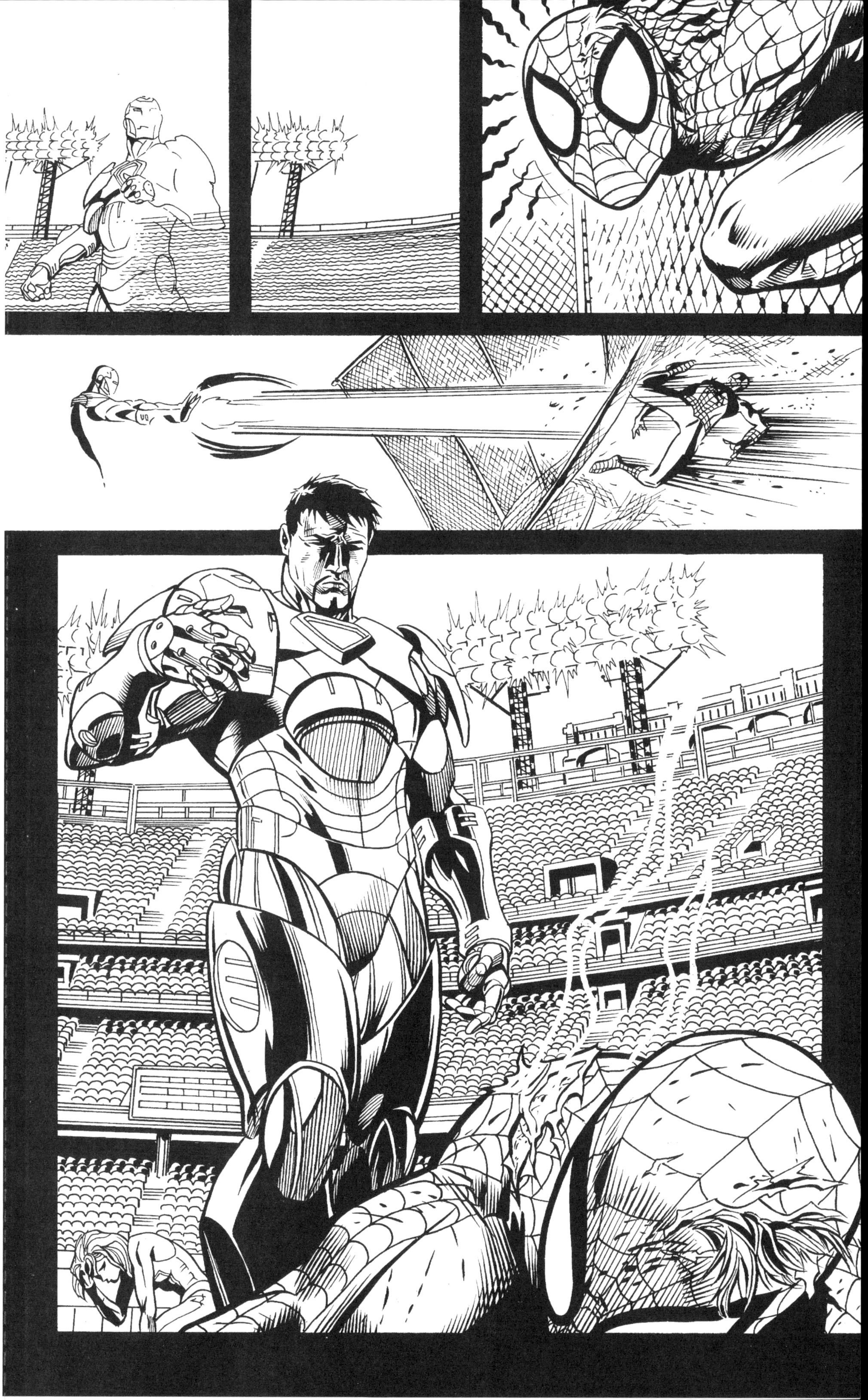

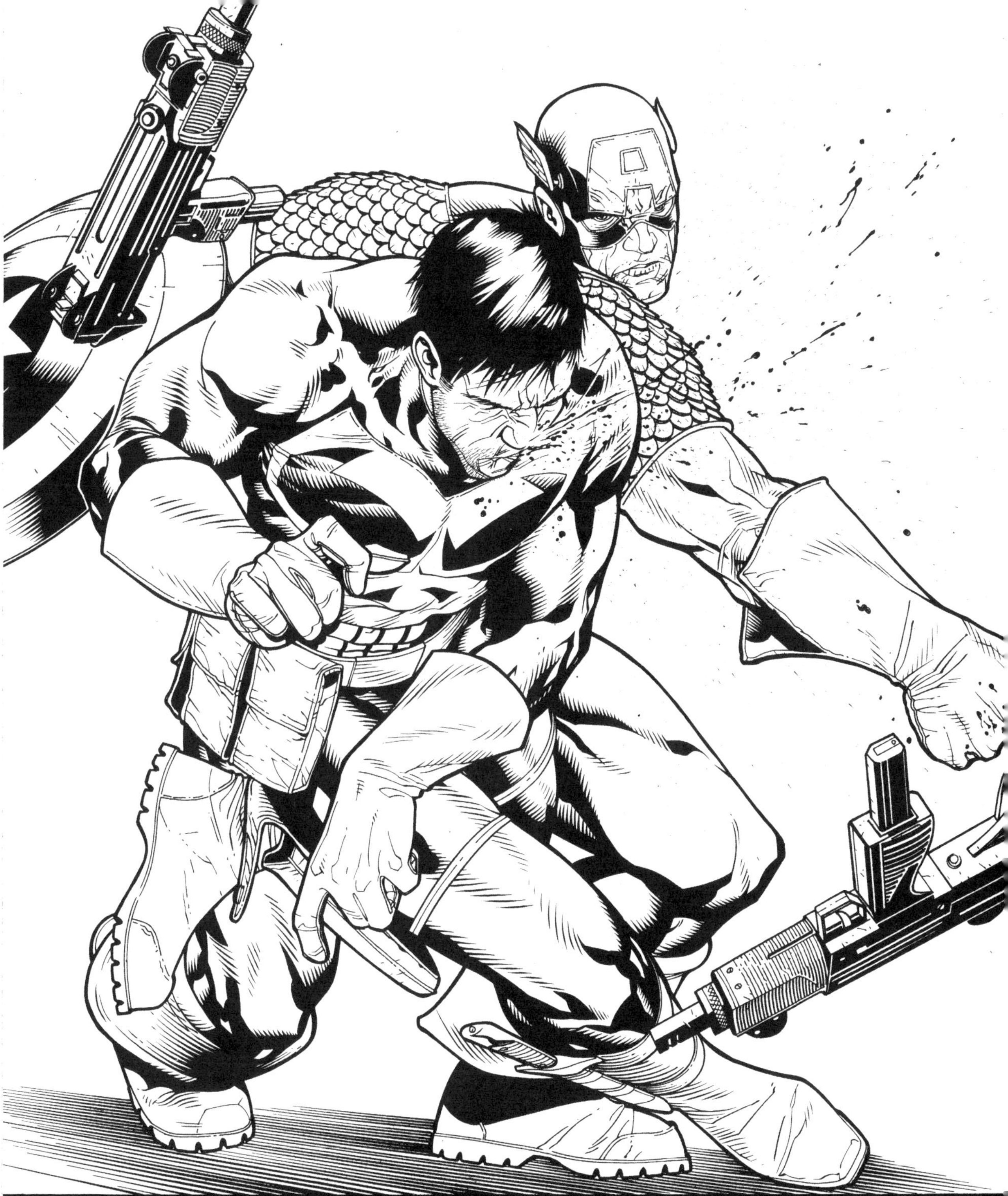
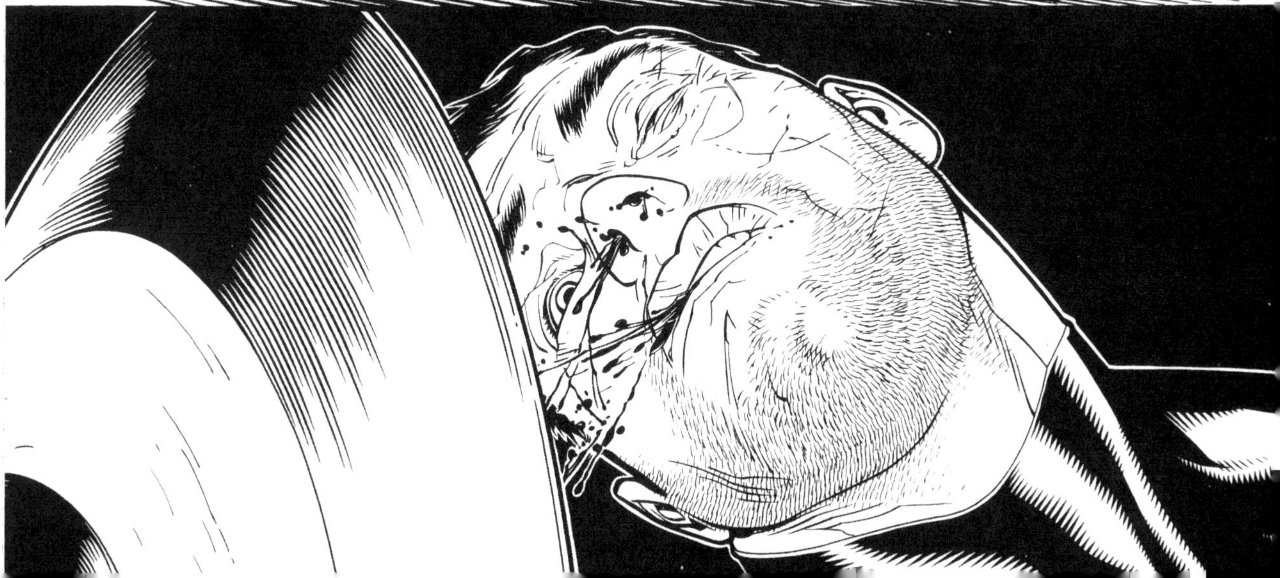

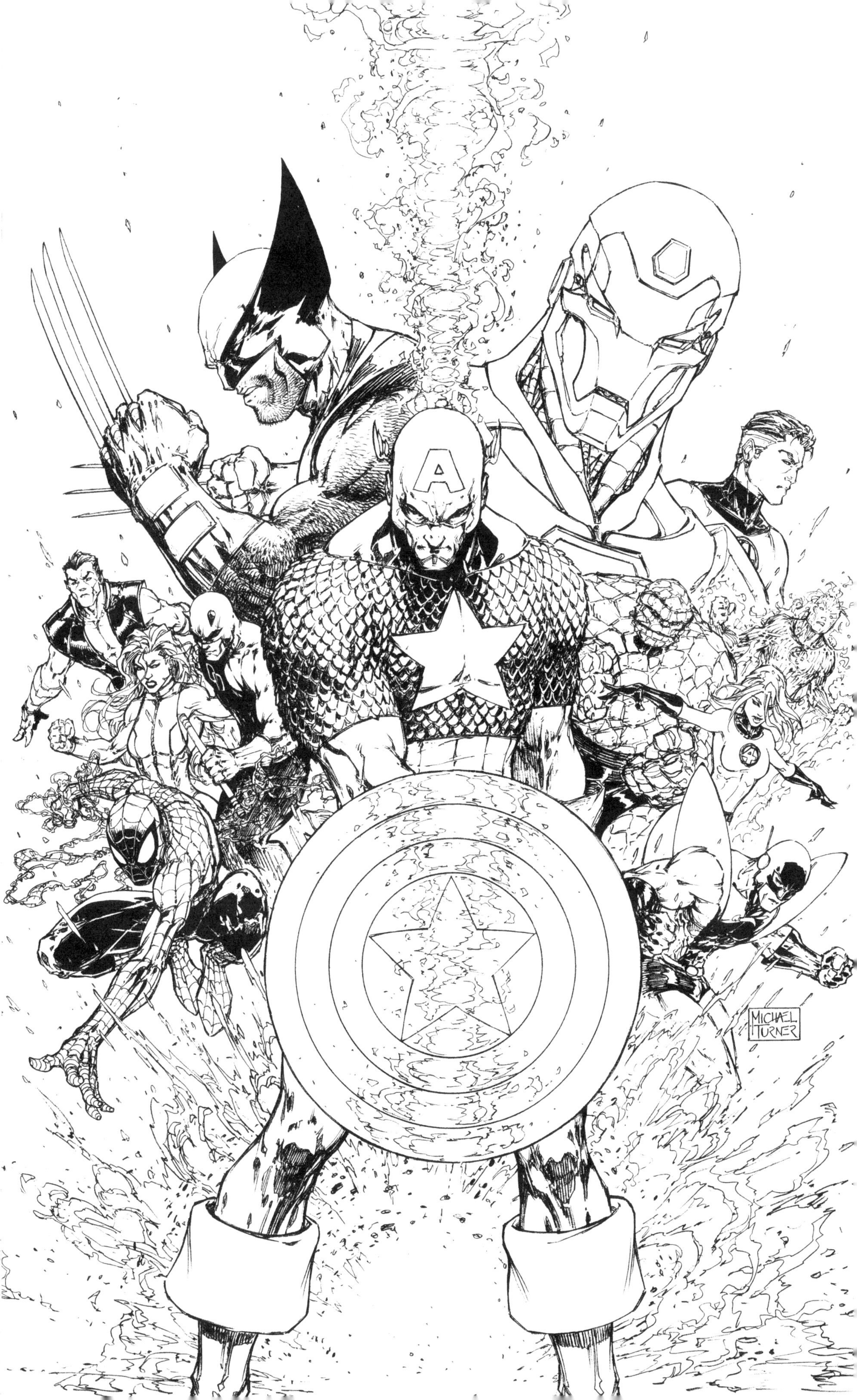
MICHAEL TURNER

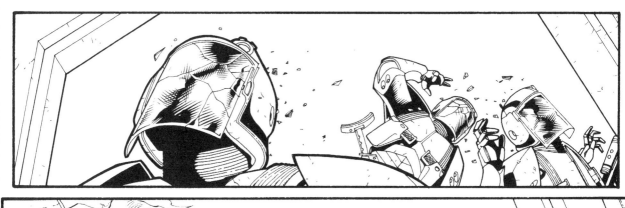

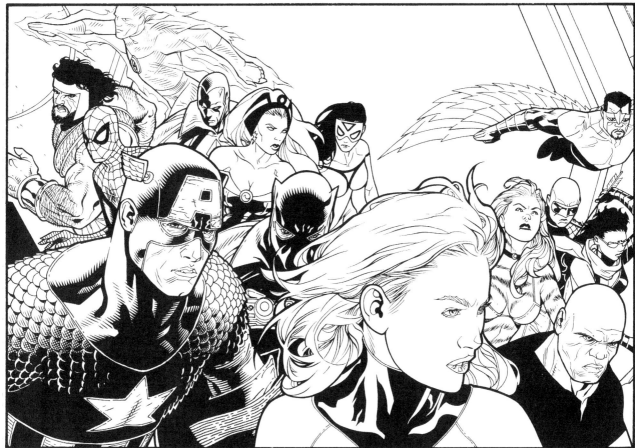

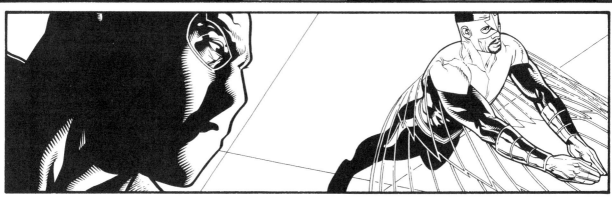

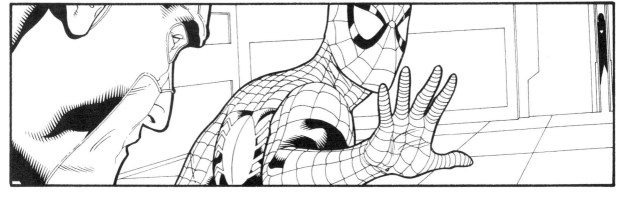

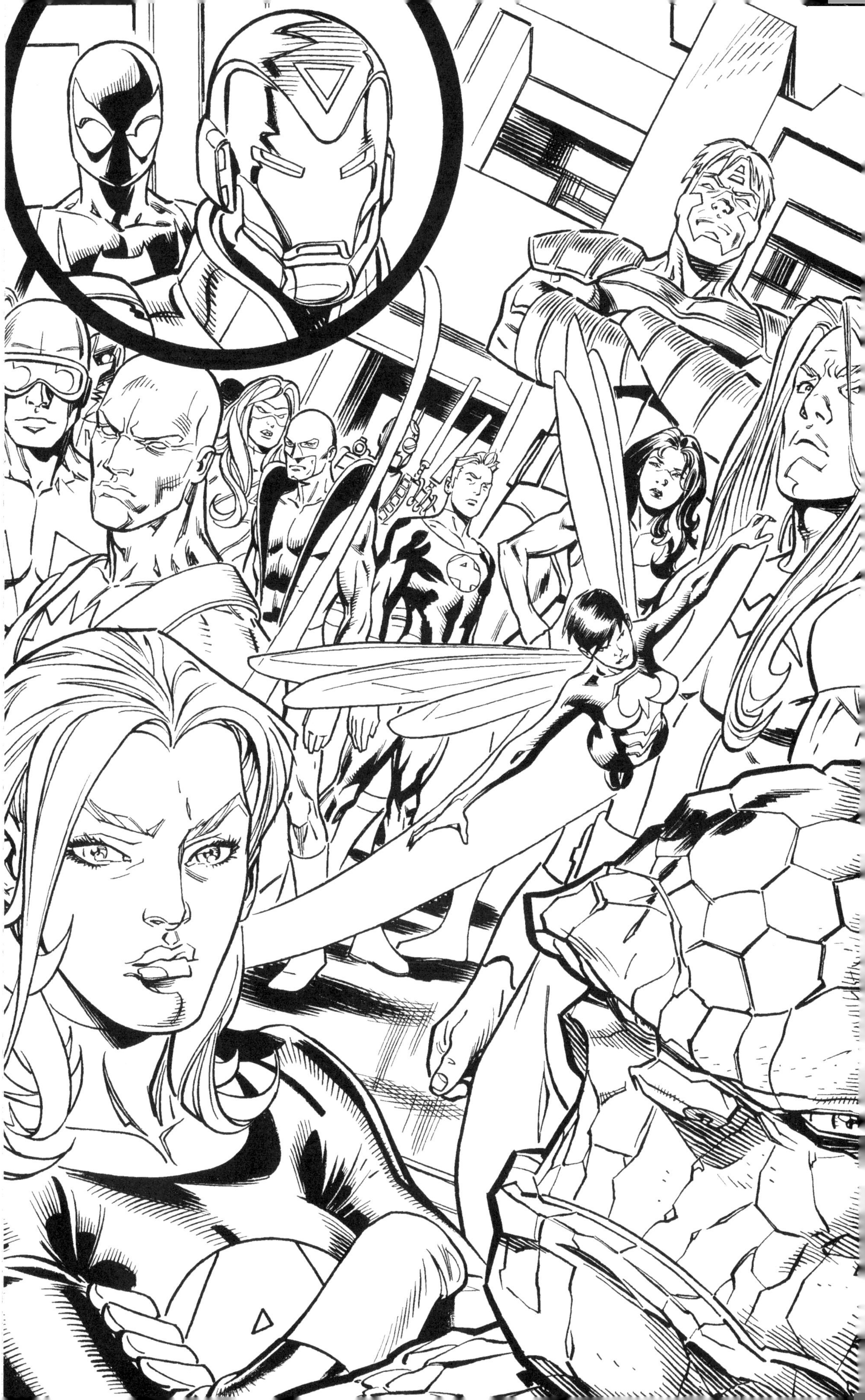

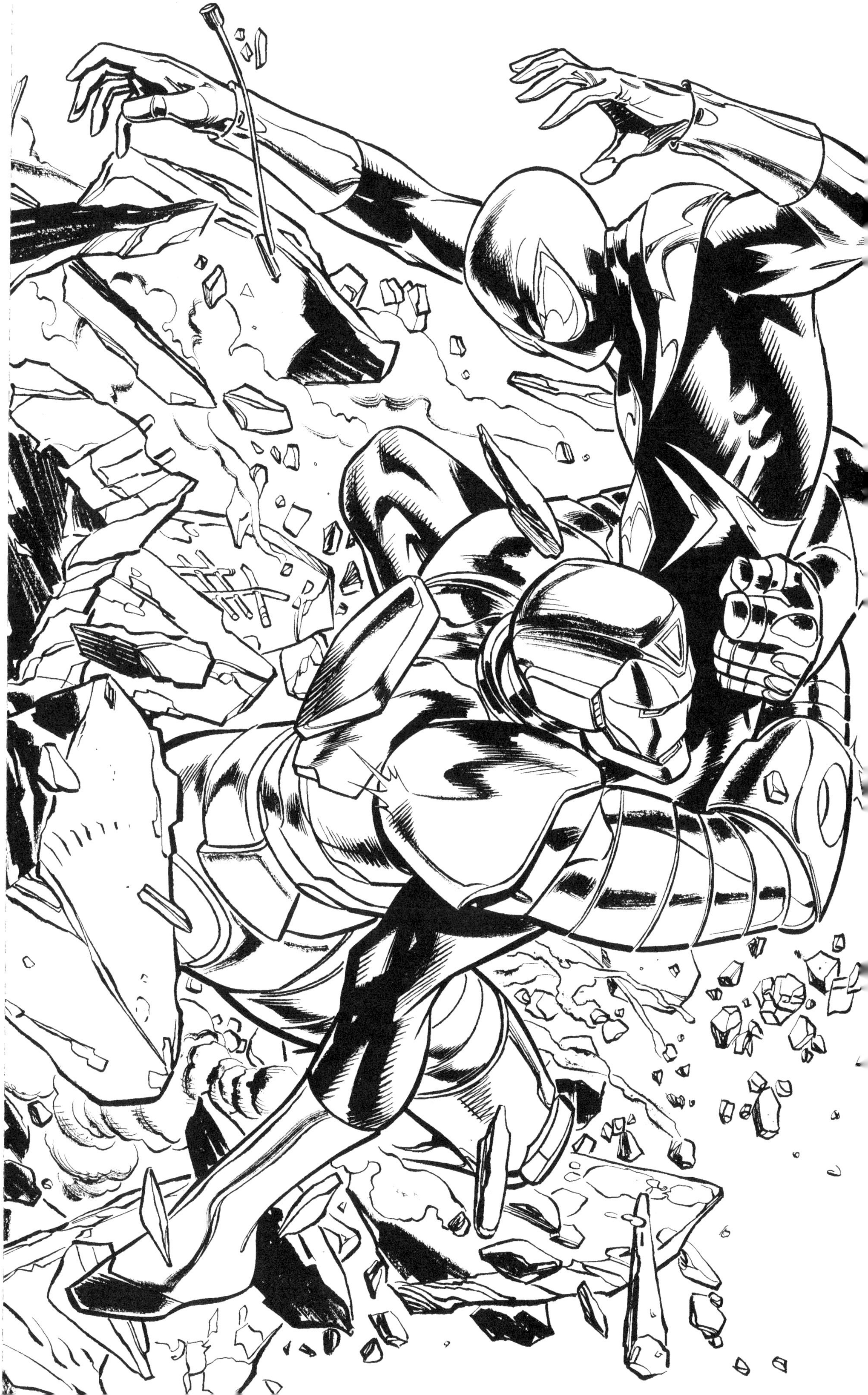

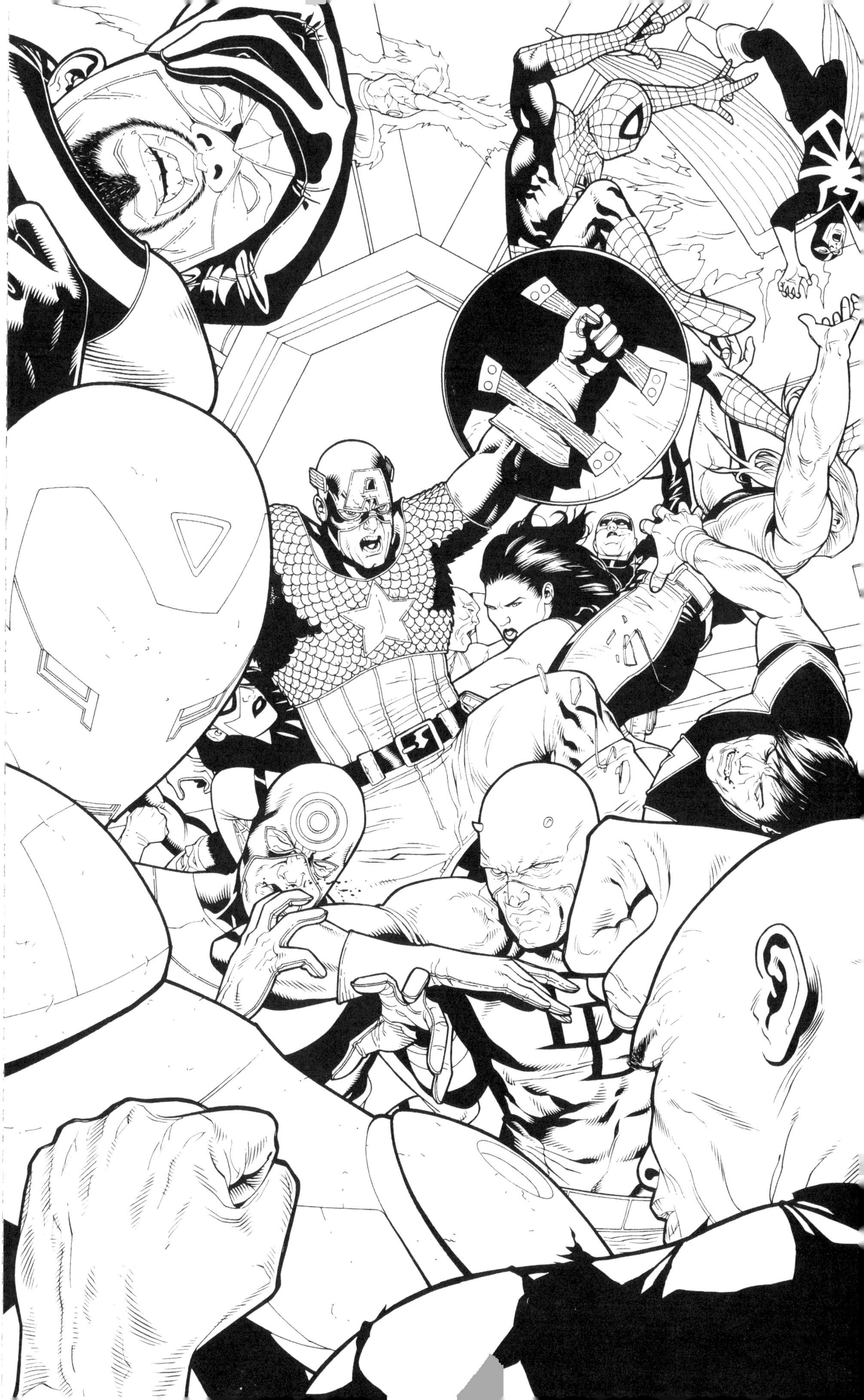

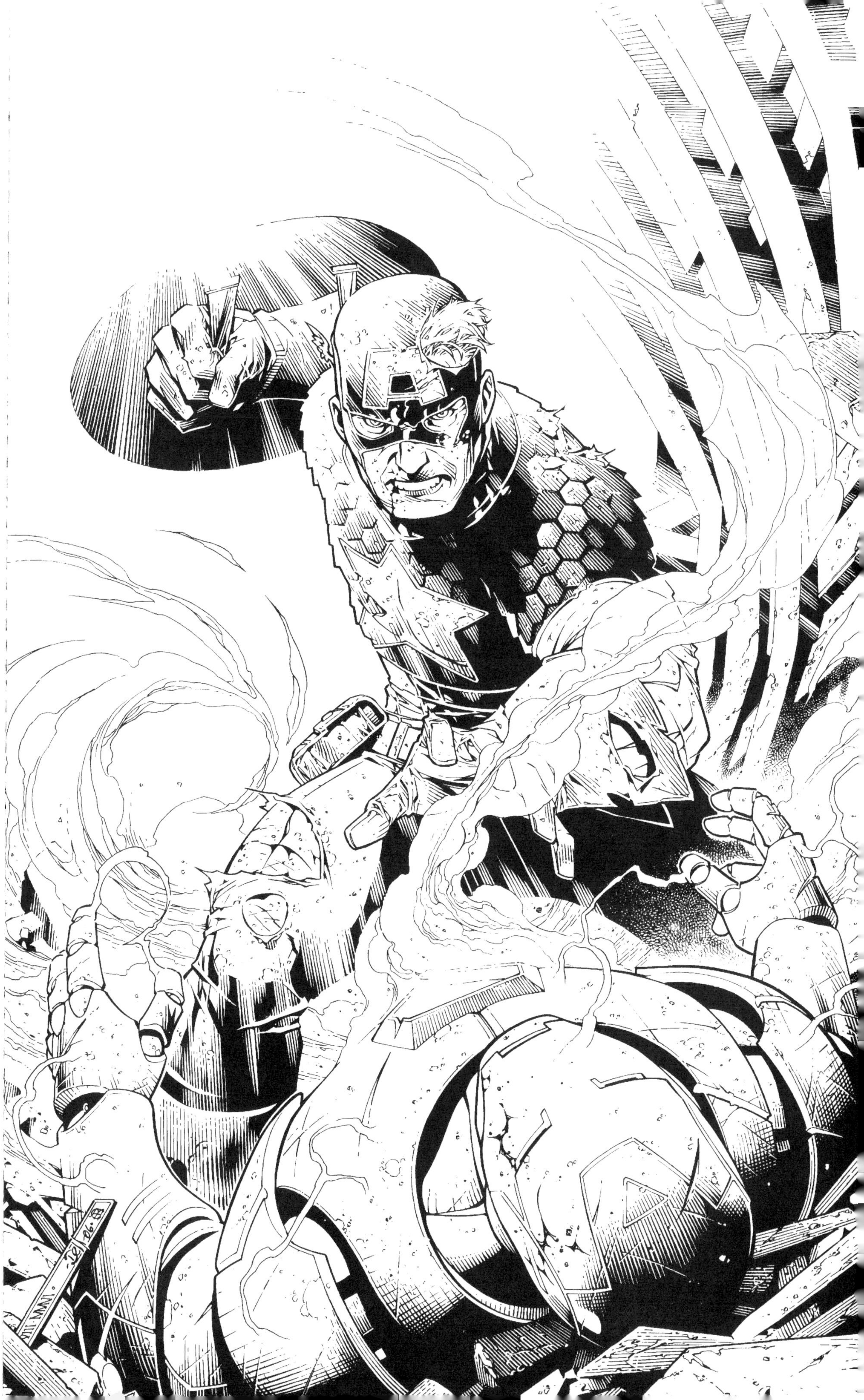

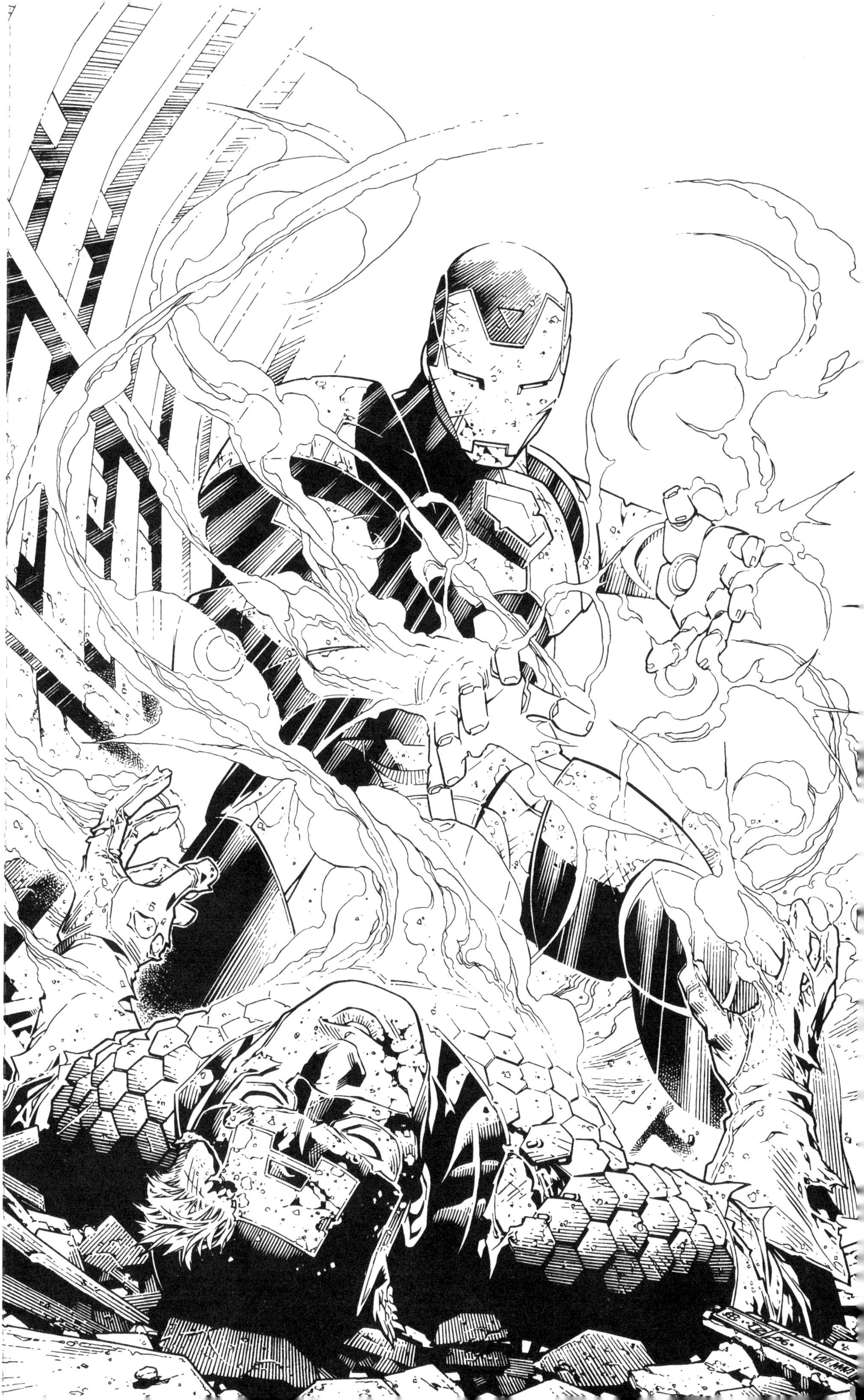

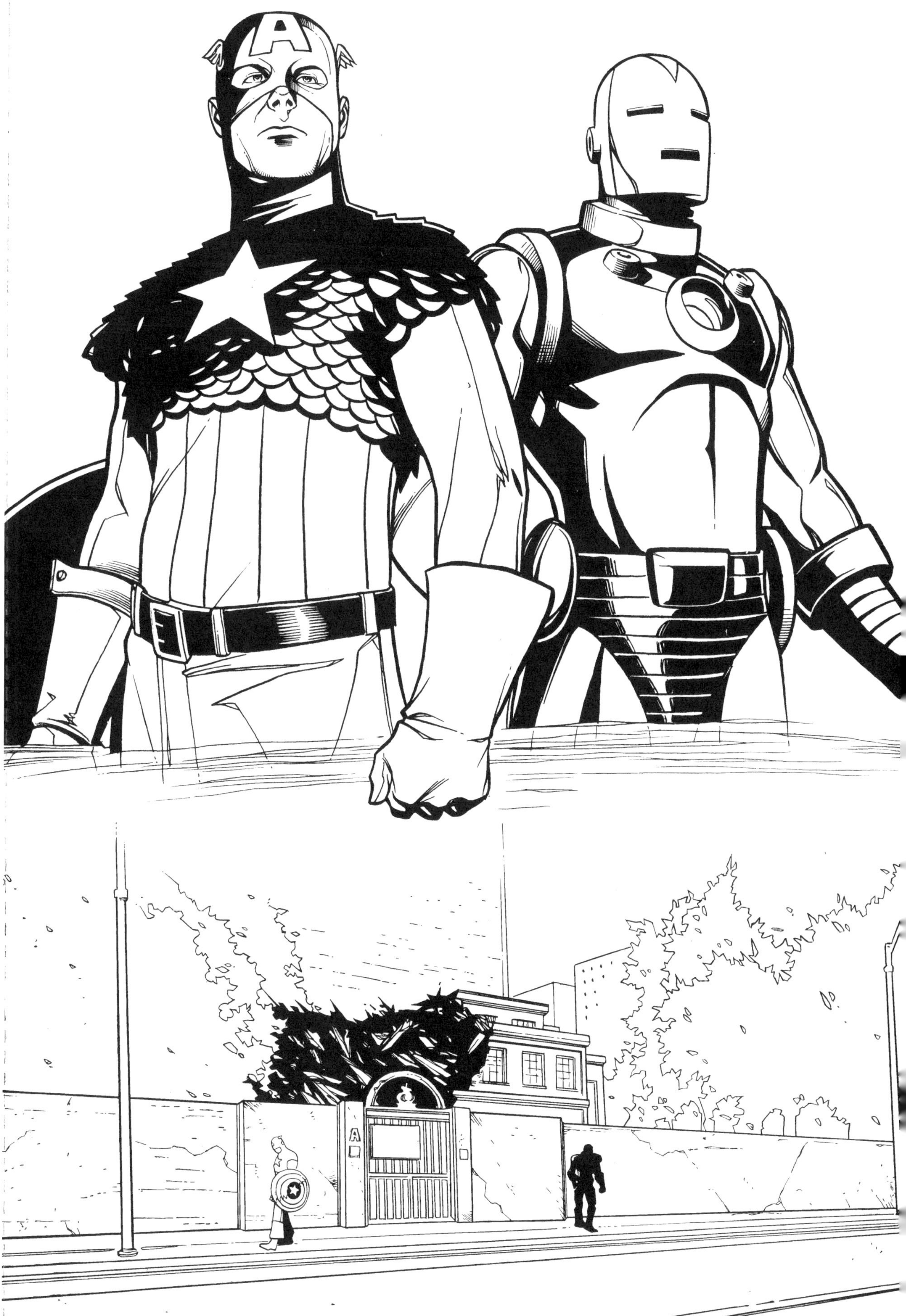

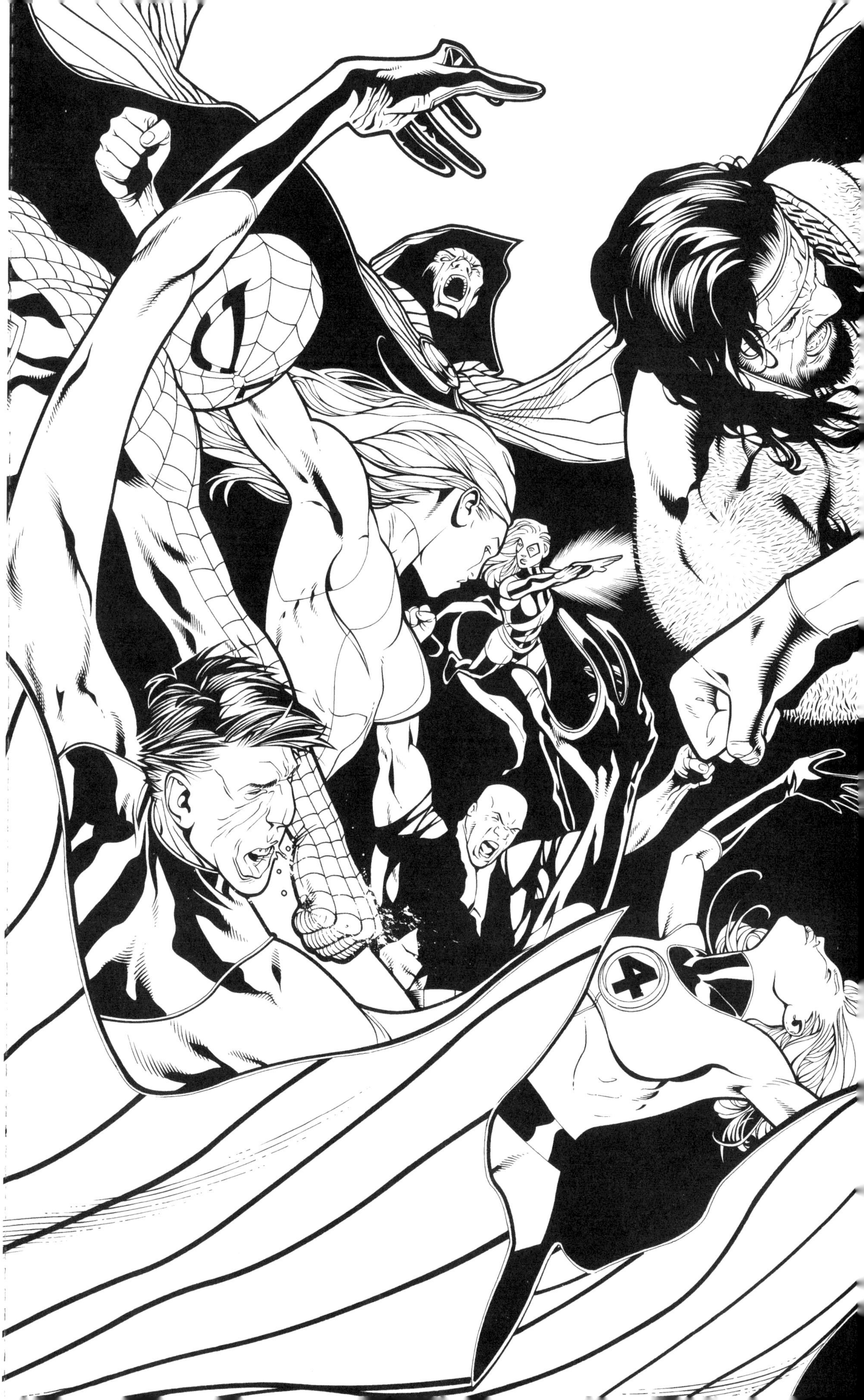

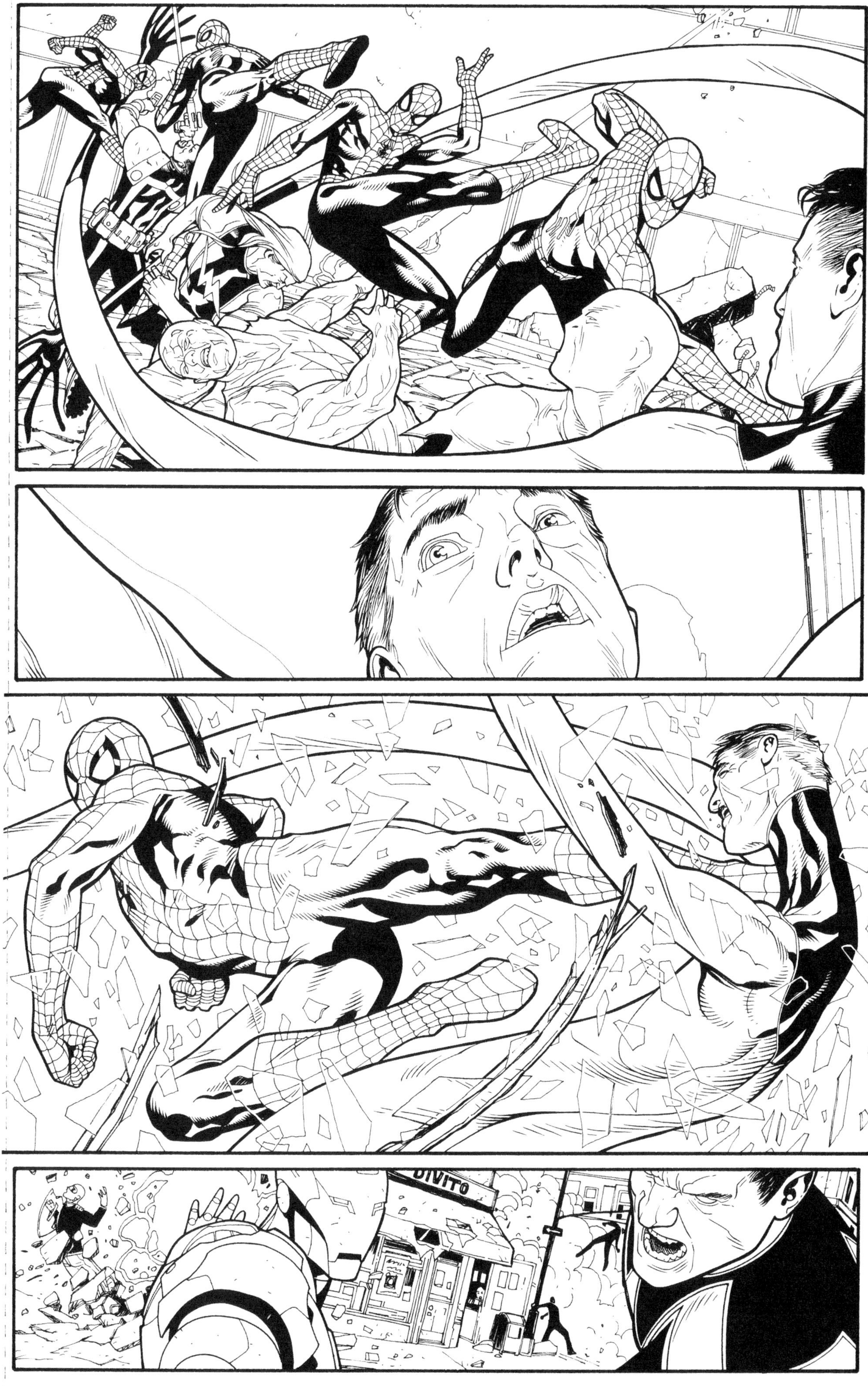
DIVITO

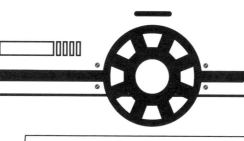

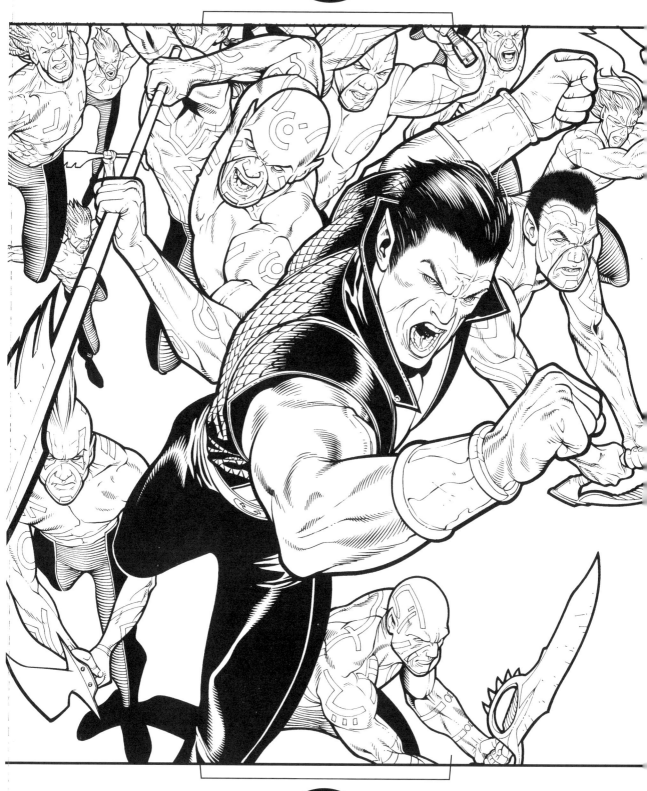

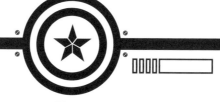

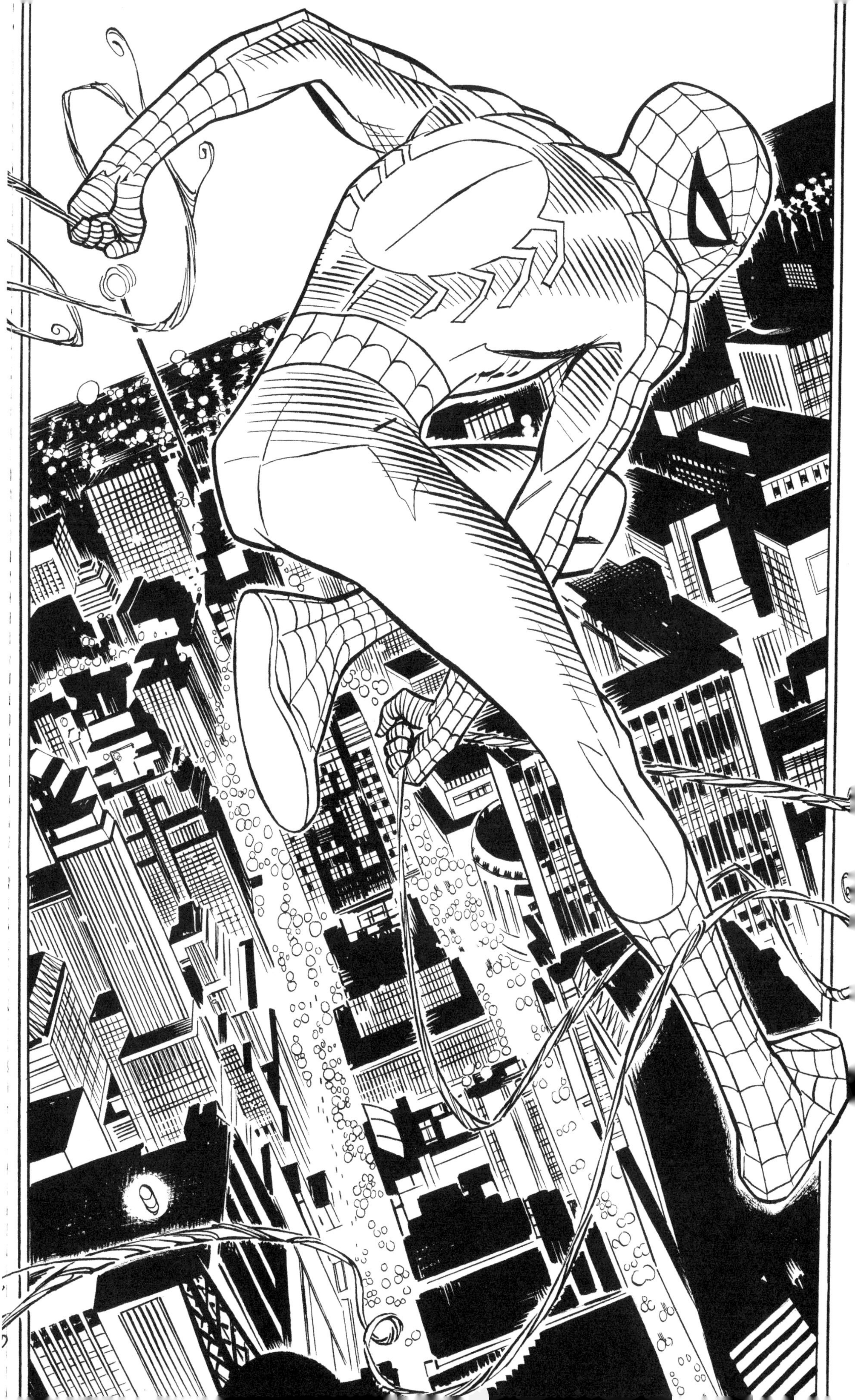

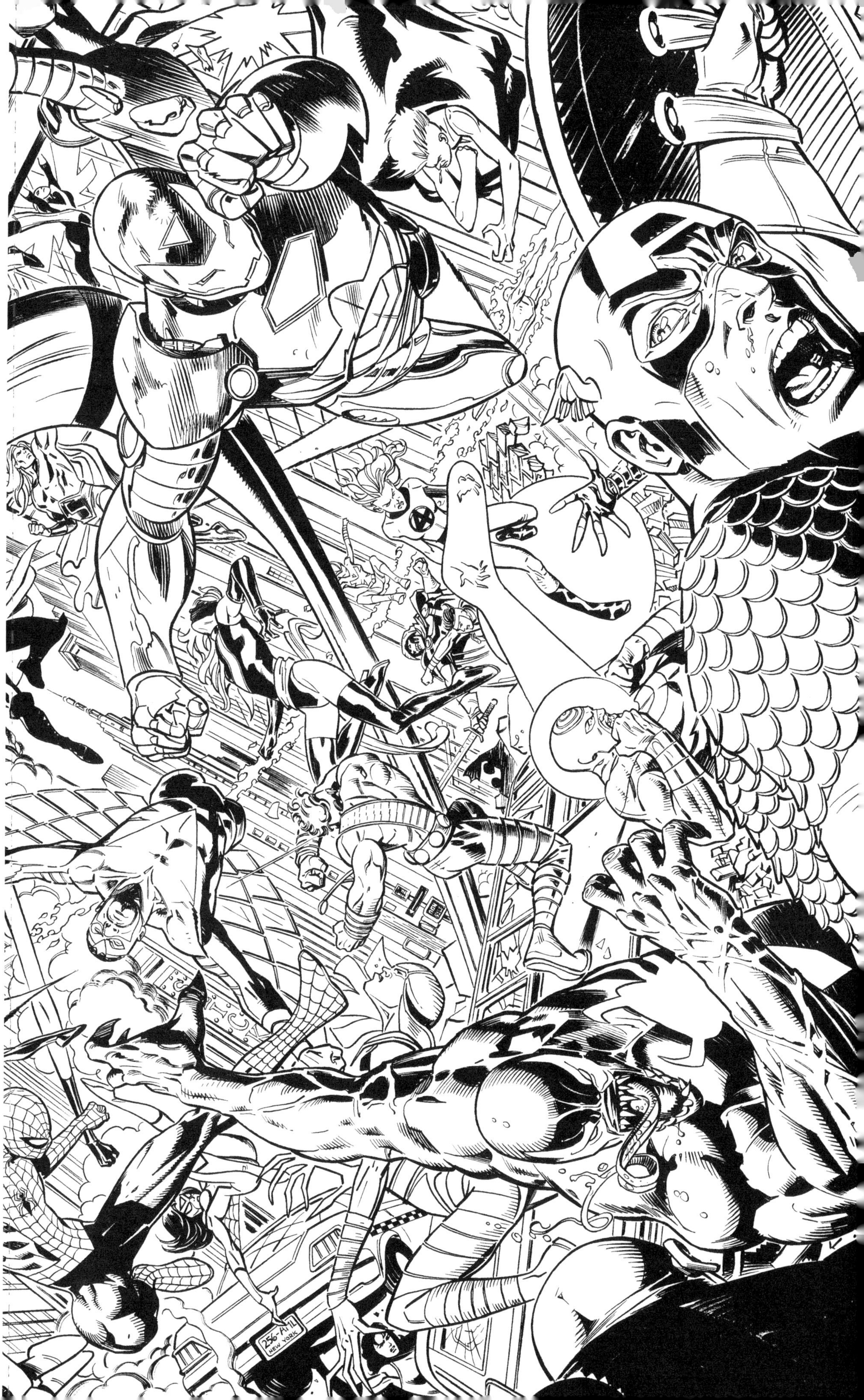
NEW YORK

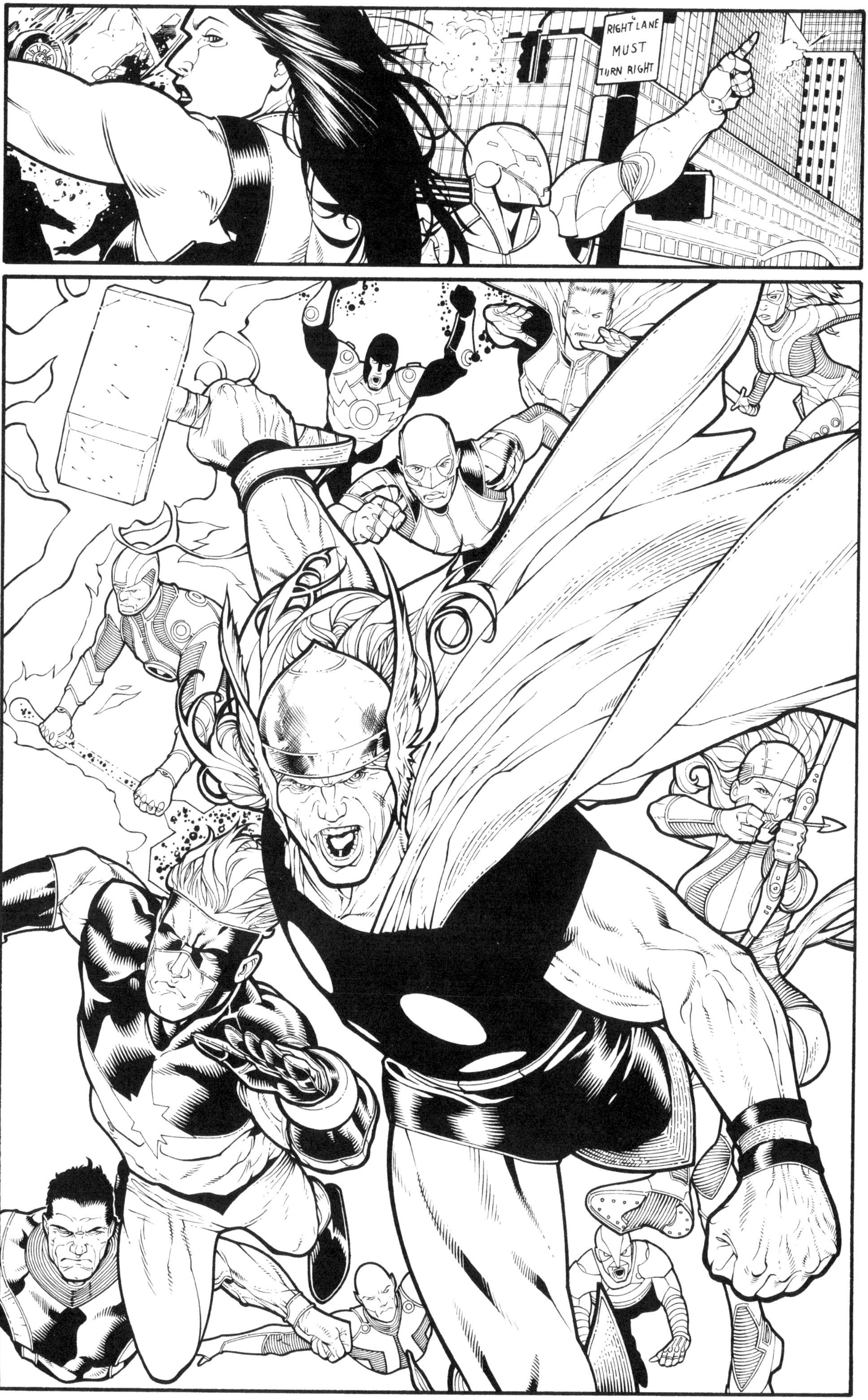
RIGHT LANE MUST TURN RIGHT

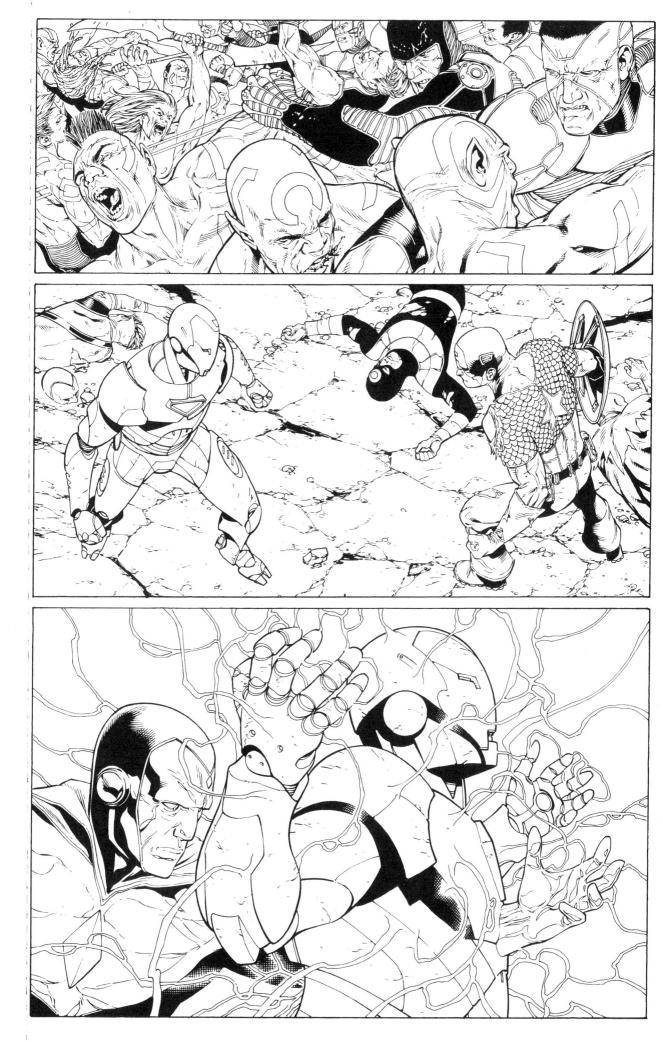

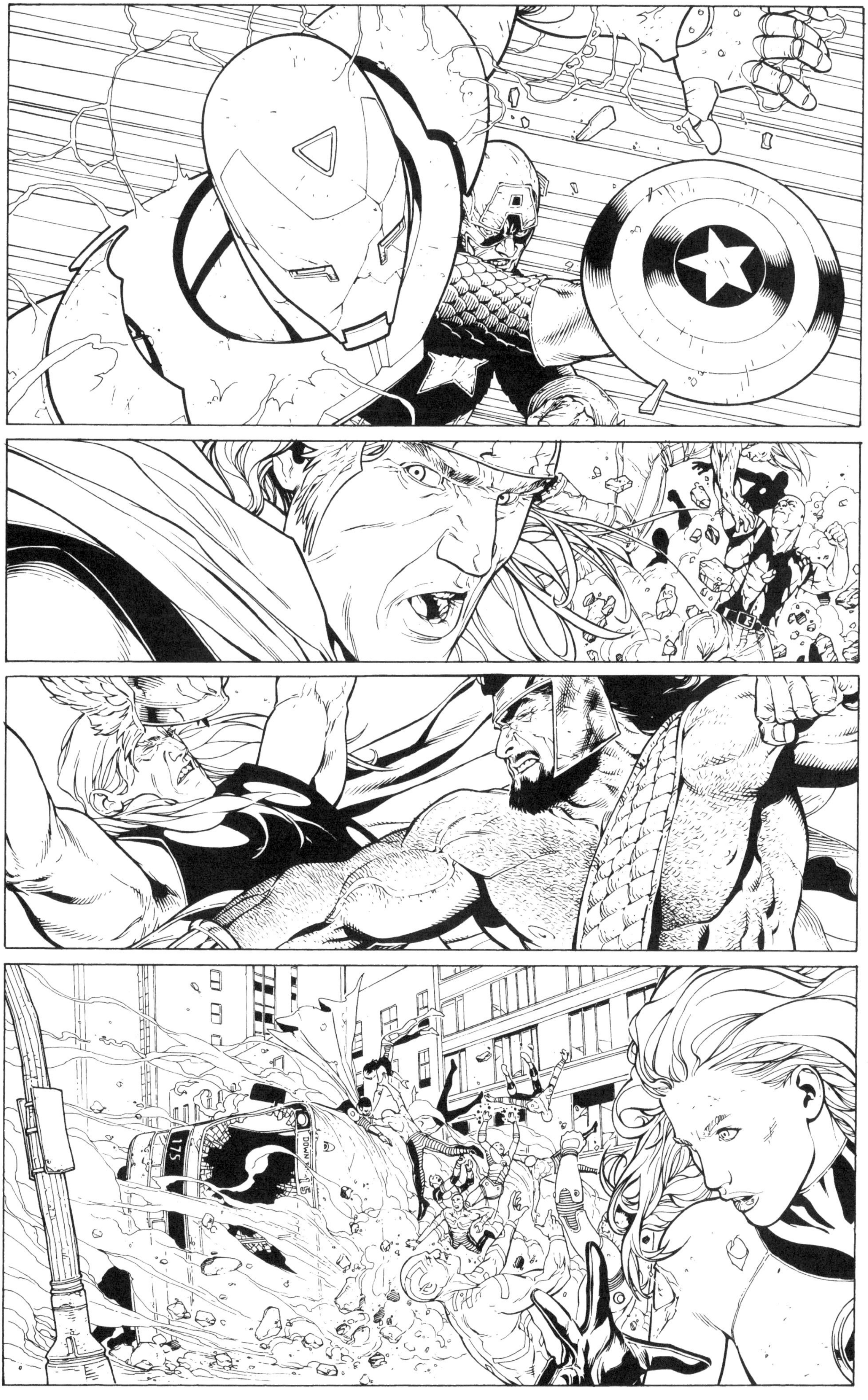
175

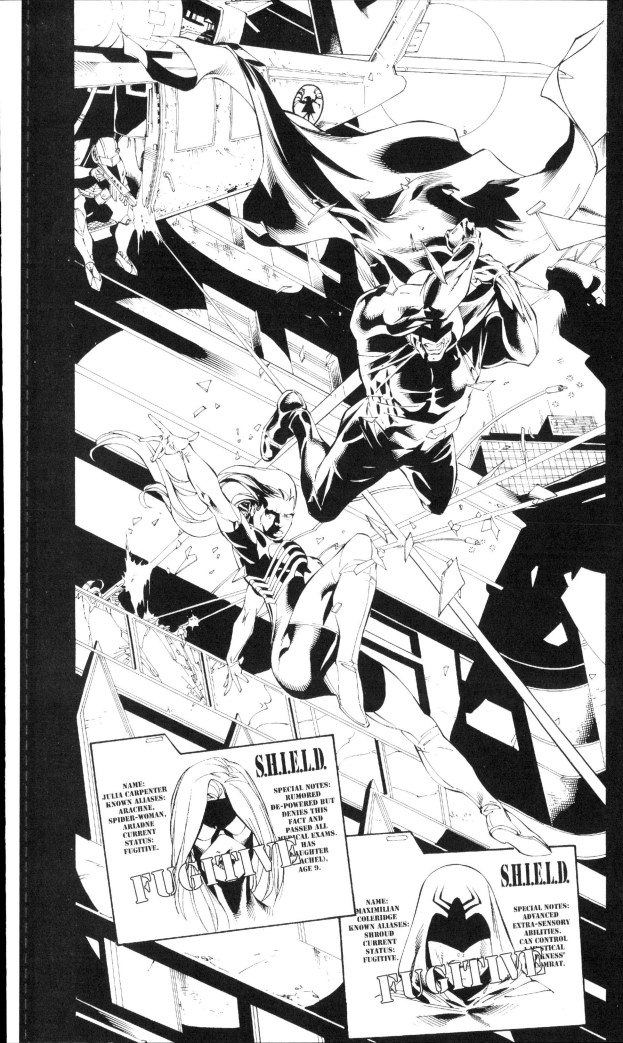

S.H.I.E.L.D.

NAME:
JULIA CARPENTER
KNOWN ALIASES:
ARACHNE,
SPIDER-WOMAN,
ARIADNE
CURRENT
STATUS:
FUGITIVE.

SPECIAL NOTES:
RUMORED
DE-POWERED BUT
DENIES THIS
FACT AND
PASSED ALL
MEDICAL EXAMS.
HAS
DAUGHTER
(RACHEL),
AGE 9.

FUGITIVE

S.H.I.E.L.D.

NAME:
MAXIMILIAN
COLERIDGE
KNOWN ALIASES:
SHROUD
CURRENT
STATUS:
FUGITIVE.

SPECIAL NOTES:
ADVANCED
EXTRA-SENSORY
ABILITIES.
CAN CONTROL
A MYSTICAL
"DARKNESS"
IN COMBAT.

FUGITIVE

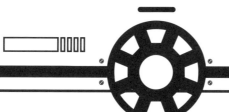

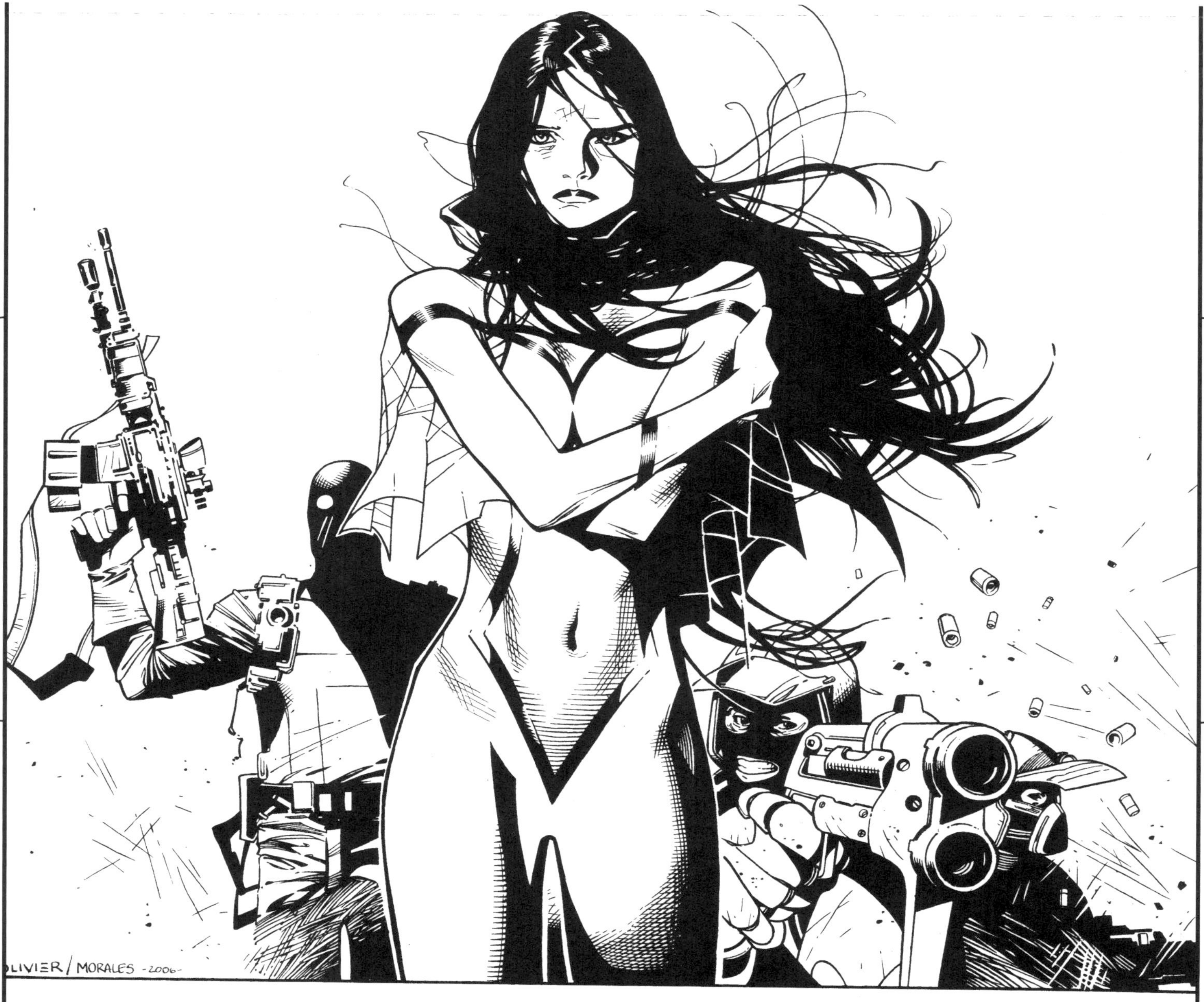
OLIVIER/MORALES -2006-

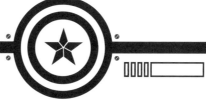

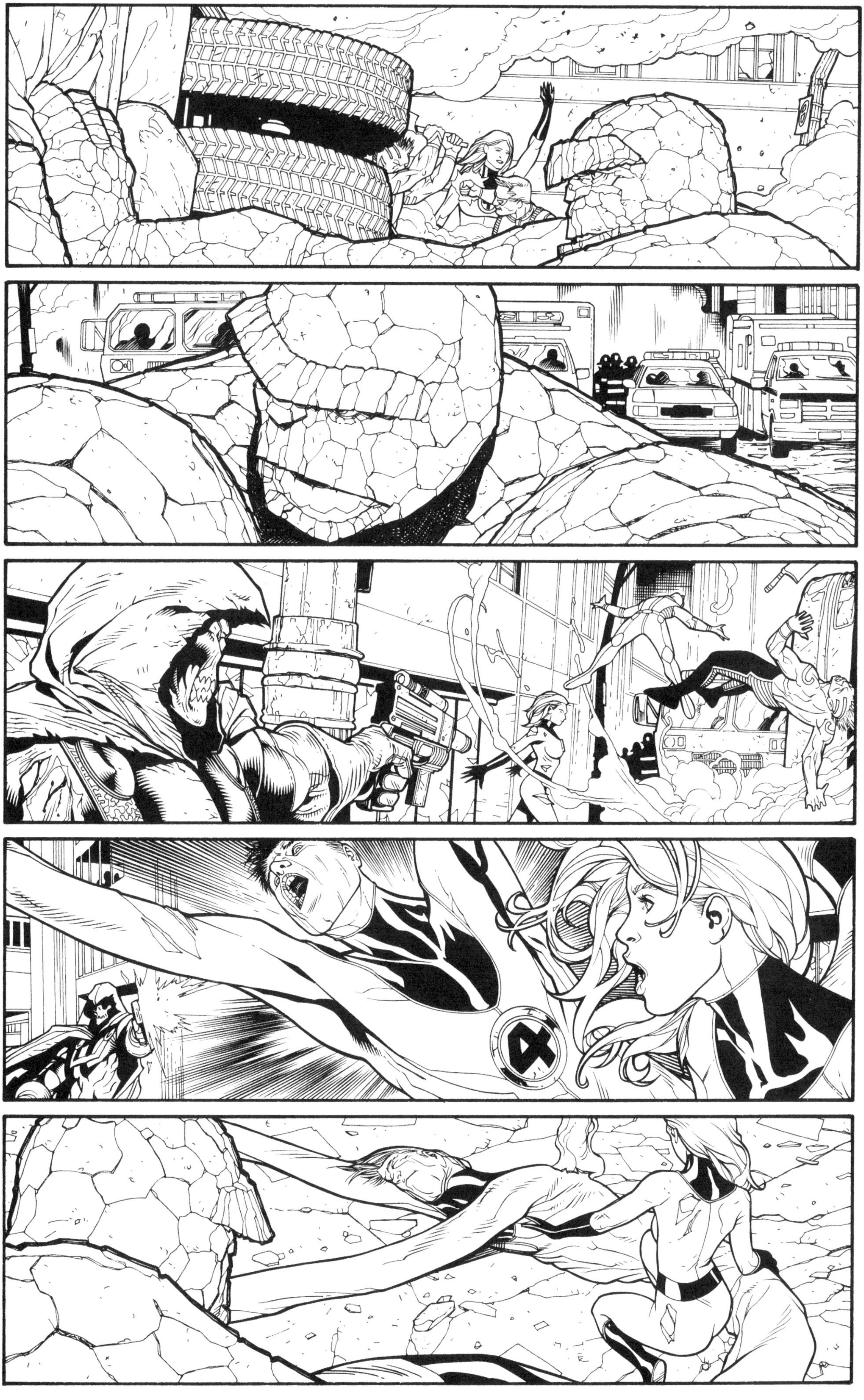

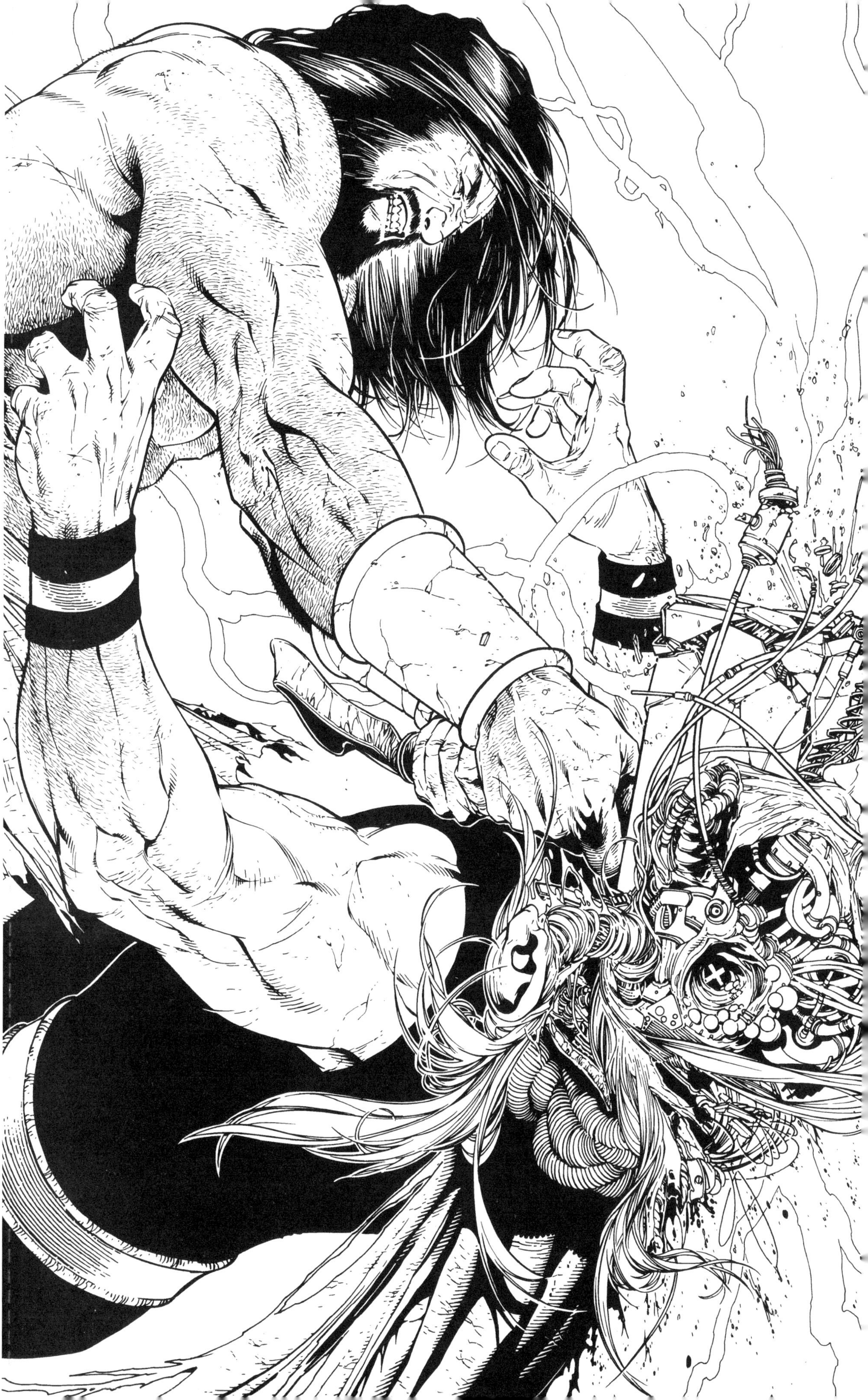

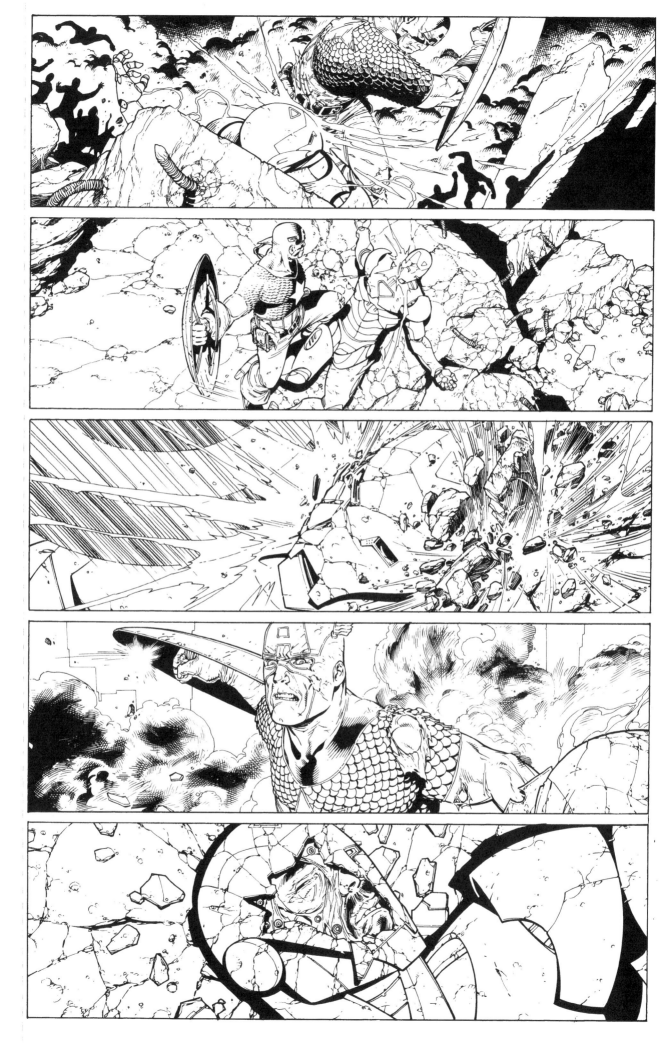

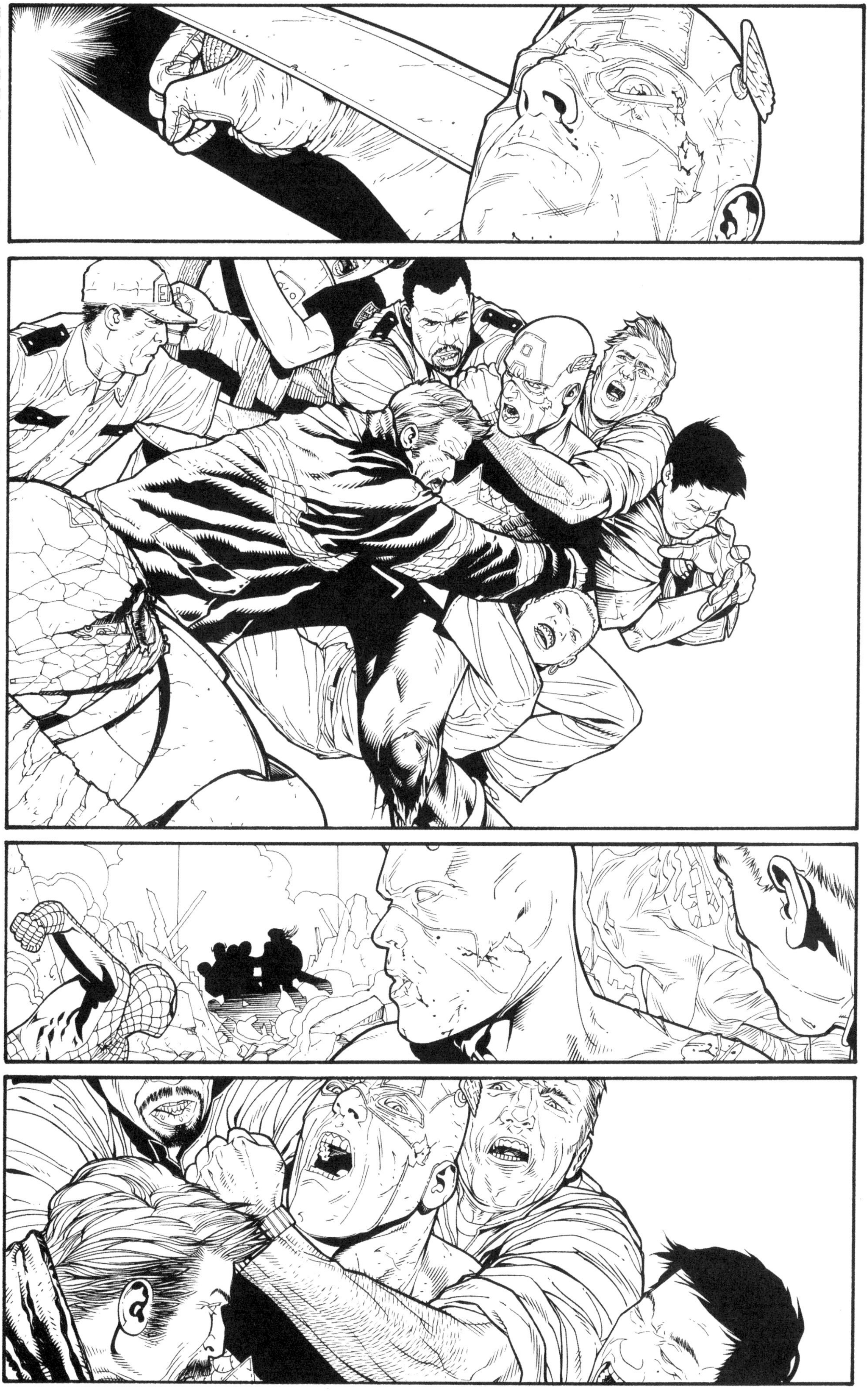

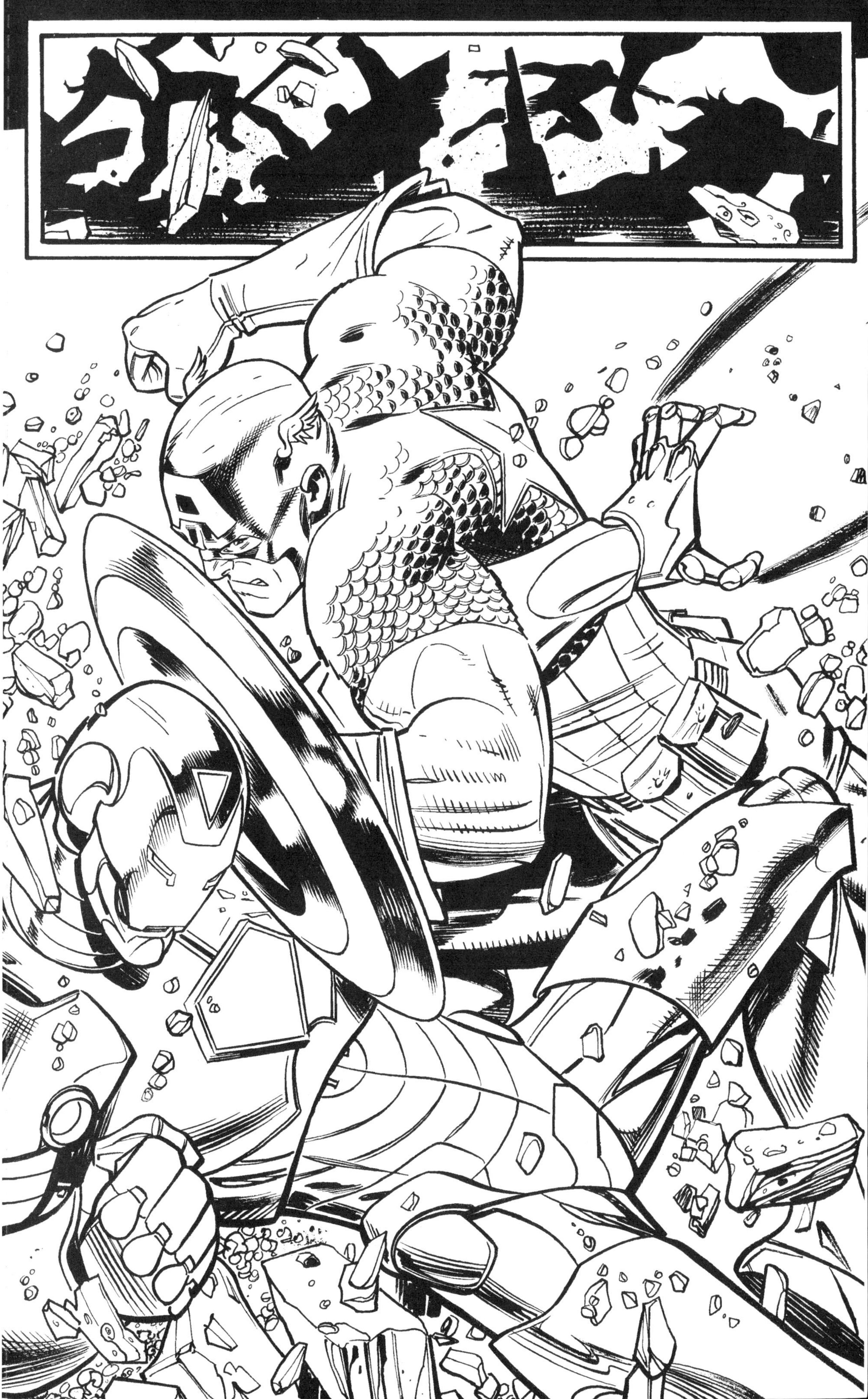

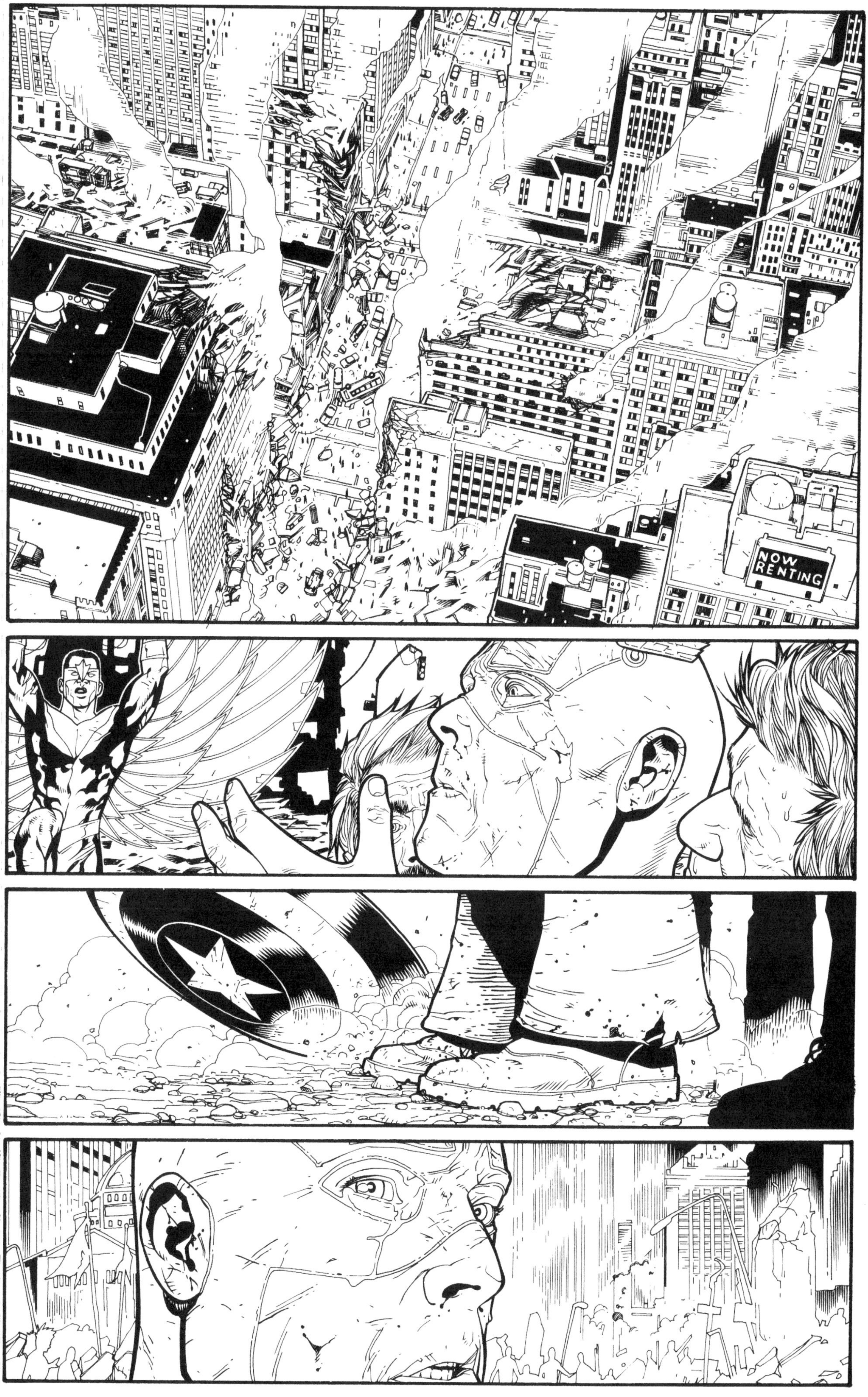
NOW RENTING

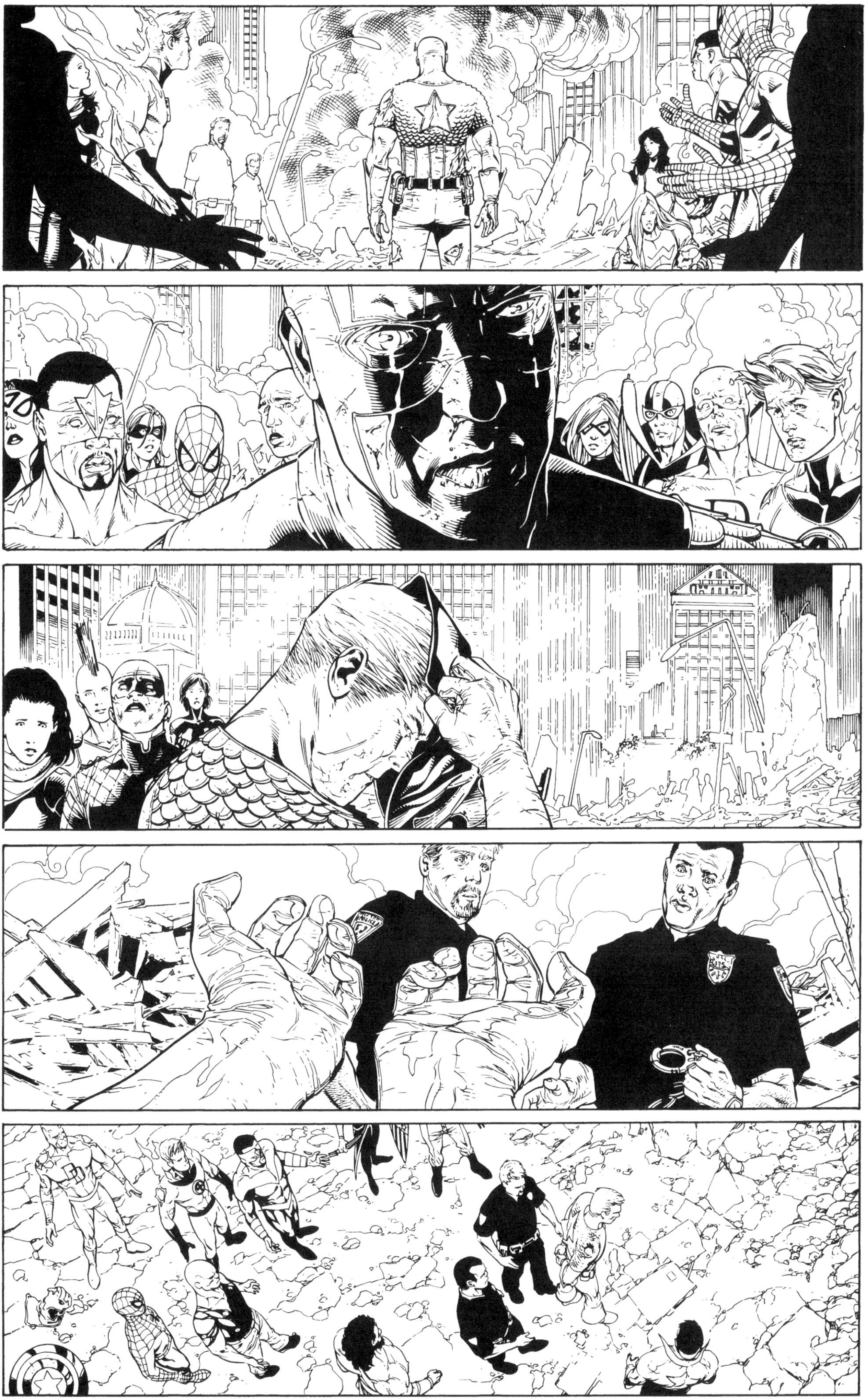

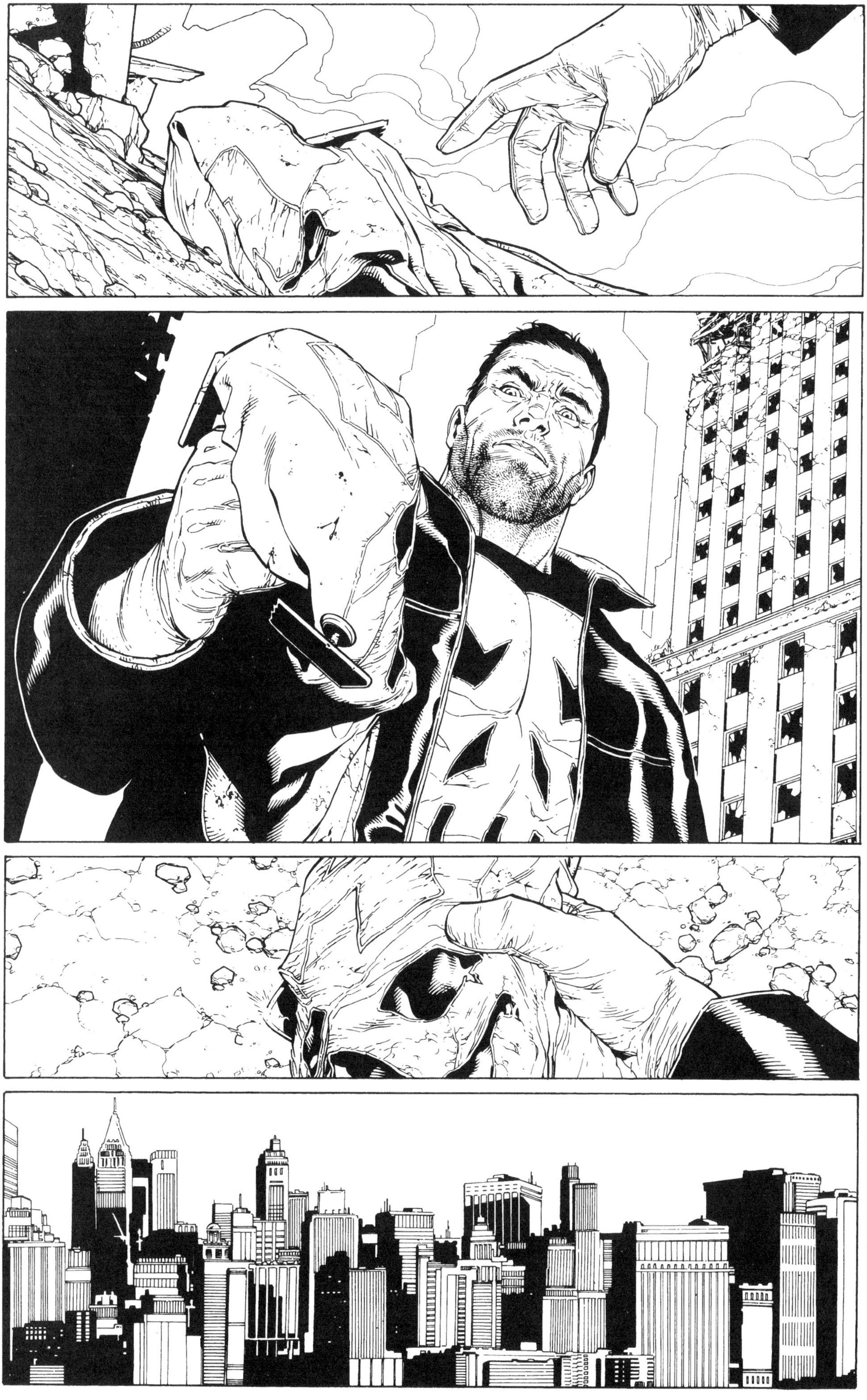

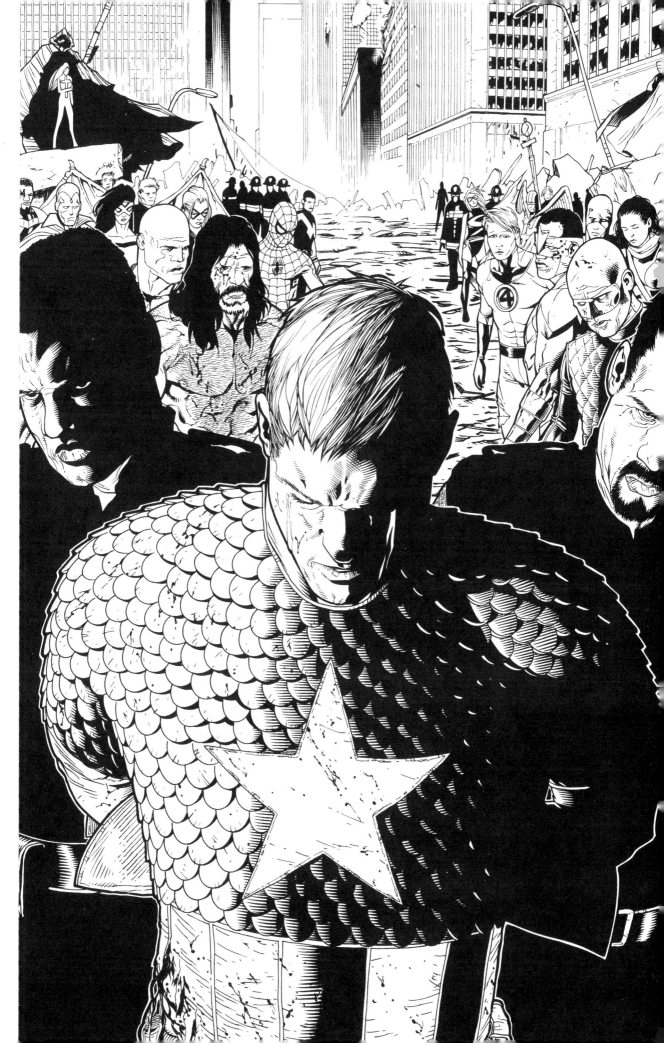